The Art of Reassembly

The Art of Reassembly

A MEMOIR OF EARLY MOTHER LOSS AND AFTERGRIEF

PEG CONWAY

SHE WRITES PRESS

Published 2021

Printed in the United States of America

Print ISBN: 978-1-64742-215-8
E-ISBN: 978-1-64742-216-5
Library of Congress Control Number: 2021910757

For information, address:
She Writes Press
1569 Solano Ave #546
Berkeley, CA 94707

She Writes Press is a division of SparkPoint Studio, LLC.

For Mary Lee Wimberg Morse
March 20, 1933–November 5, 1970

In loving memory

"The Aftergrief is where we learn to live with a central paradox of bereavement: that a loss can recede in time yet remain so exquisitely present."

—Hope Edelman

Prologue

The unraveling began after we finished dinner at a Thai place in Lincoln Park. Our young adult son, his girlfriend, and another friend—all Chicago residents—had joined my husband and me for a drink at our hotel's rooftop bar before riding together to the restaurant. After our feast of sushi, stir-fry, and bottles of wine, I expected more chatting outside during the wait for separate transportation, a relaxed goodbye that would manage tectonic shifts beneath the surface. Two weeks earlier, Michael had informed us that he and Madeline would be moving in together this summer when their current leases expire. Though a minor geographic change, symbolically it widened the distance from our home in Cincinnati.

Instead, following dinner, I had barely left the restaurant when a random cab appeared at the curb. Madeline turned to Michael and said, "Should we just take this?" In the next instant, they hugged us in thanks and piled in the back seat. Michael waved and said, "See you tomorrow!" as the cab pulled away. Suddenly void of their youthful vibrancy, the neighborhood became sinister.

Just as abruptly, my switch flipped. My body taut, I launched a tirade about their hasty exit. "Leaving us alone on the street corner!"

"They probably thought our Uber was on the way," Joe said, his face angled to his phone as he tapped out a ride request.

Perhaps, a tiny corner of my brain suggested, they treated us as they would their friends, assuming competence to summon our own ride after dining out in a big city. Pacing the sidewalk, I couldn't listen to that rational voice, not yet. Finally, our driver did a U-turn to pull up in front of us. Back in our room soon after, still I huffed and puffed, until suddenly the frenzy deflated like a balloon. I did not want negativity to define the evening or ruin the next day, the final one of our trip before returning home.

During our afternoon with Michael, Joe and I had attended a middle school boys' basketball game at a YMCA where he and his friend coached. The impetus for our weekend trip was to witness this part of his life, where the pounding of the basketballs on the gym floor, the loud whine of the horn, the piercing tweet of the referee's whistle, all of it had mirrored Michael's grade school playing days. Madeline had joined us in the row of metal folding chairs by the sidelines partway through the first half, and we chatted easily for the rest of the game. Though down by fifteen at the half, Michael's guys had gone on to win by four in overtime, a major accomplishment for them. On the way out, we had struck up a conversation with the parents on our left.

"Who is your child on the team?" they had queried.

Our response—"The coach!"—had evoked chuckles all around, but for me the levity had landed heavily, like a weight on my chest. I enjoyed watching basketball when Michael was involved. It was something we had shared during his growing up. Now it wasn't the same. He was out of college, working, living his own life. Joe and I were truly just spectators. Naturally, things evolved as Michael became an adult. In theory, I hoped that he would find someone to share his life, but this juncture had arrived sooner and in a different manner than expected. It was normal, but I struggled.

"Ooohh," I whimpered aloud now in the hotel room, recognizing at last the familiar emotional flashover that occurred whenever circumstances pressed on an old wound. Whether it was being the last to leave a social gathering or watching a beloved child flourish independently, the reaction was the same, always a reverberation of early mother loss. An outburst was triggered, followed by self-recrimination, and then trembling vulnerability as the acute phase ebbed. Joe glanced over from the closet where he was hanging up his coat, eyebrows raised, questioning.

"Will you please hold me?" I said in a near whisper.

As he hugged me close, wordlessly, our physical contact broke the spell. Hot tears spilled down my cheeks. My breathing slowed. My muscles loosened. I returned to the present, knitted back into relationships, embracing a kinder self-understanding. *It's okay. It's always part of you. Just let it be there. You're okay. Breathe.*

PART ONE

Chapter One

Sweat prickled my neck and back as I entered the cafeteria line with my second-grade class on that September day. In vain, I lifted a tray from the stack and scanned the faces behind the counter. My voice pitch rose in tandem with my anxiety when I asked the person who dished up my plate, "Where's my mom? I thought she was coming today."

She shook her head, though her expression was kind as she replied, "She didn't show up. She's not here."

I had been clinging to my mom's expected presence on lunch volunteer duty as a life raft of normality, but now it floated away from my grasp. I ate my meatloaf and mashed potatoes without tasting them, tingling with dread, while attempting to keep up with the chatter of my classmates. That afternoon when I arrived home, I learned that my mom had fainted in the kitchen and, upon discovering her there, my little brother Tim, age five, immediately set out to find me at school. We lived more than two miles away, most of it a major four-lane thoroughfare. Not far off our street as Tim walked up this busy road, barefoot, a police car stopped. Tim explained his mission, and the police officer drove him home, where Mom had come to and was sitting at the kitchen table.

I wonder now how much time had elapsed and what was crossing her mind. Did she realize Tim was gone? She was taken to the hospital, and it was determined she'd had a seizure, diagnosed as epilepsy. But my mom was a nurse and knew that was ridiculous, my aunt told me many years later. Mom had asked her younger sister to fetch her medical books and figured out for herself that the breast cancer, diagnosed two years earlier, was spreading to her brain. Her illness occurred several years before chemotherapy was used to treat the disease.

Mom stayed in the hospital for several days. My grandma was already coming over regularly. After her collapse, Mom no longer got dressed. Instead, she wore a knee-length, short-sleeved housecoat that snapped up the front, made of white cotton with tiny black dots, with a round collar and two square pockets in front. Sometimes she stayed in bed, and once I saw her throw up the sandwich she had just eaten into a napkin. Her skin was pale, her once-coiffed hair flattened to her head, and she was quiet. In that jewel-toned autumn, I saw only gray.

On November 6, about six weeks after the collapse, I woke to pale light in the pink-walled room I shared with my older sister and realized it was almost time to get up for school. I was still in bed when the door opened softly and my dad walked in, followed by my older brother Mike, a high school freshman, who was carrying Tim in his arms. My limbs tingled with sudden foreboding. Why was Mike still home? Why wasn't Dad wearing his shirt and tie for work? Why were they all coming into our room? Then Dad sat down between our twin beds. His distinctive wavy black hair, normally combed smoothly back from his forehead and temples, looked tousled. His blotchy face, eyes red-rimmed, made my throat constrict.

"Well, kids, we have an angel in the family," he said, his hoarse voice cracking as he finished.

"Mom?" I whispered, launching into his arms sobbing even before he nodded yes.

Soon after, displaying a child's limited capacity to absorb such enormity, I left his lap saying, "I need to get ready for school," but Dad said we would not be going to school that day.

Down in the kitchen, my mom's parents were cooking breakfast. My aunt arrived shortly after. Their being at our house on a weekday morning when I should be at school heightened the sense of wrongness. I felt afraid but lacked words to even name it. My fear existed as a void. My insides felt empty, like I was floating in space, untethered. I sat in Mike's lap sucking my thumb as the grown-ups conversed in subdued tones.

The morning of the funeral, I watched men in dark suits heave the casket from the hearse parked in the circle drive of our Catholic parish and carry it up the concrete stairs. I stood mesmerized by the slick unfolding of the metal stand where it was placed. Nearly unable to breathe as I walked down the aisle in the procession amid the booming organ music, my limbs again tingling, I caught the familiar faces of my classmates all seated together in the first few pews of the far-left section. A flash of pleasure was followed by a funny feeling that I could not yet name, the opening line of an inner narrative in which being motherless set me apart from other kids, somehow defective in a basic way. Into the vast and eternal silence of my mother's absence, I felt myself falling, falling, falling. Where would I land? I had never known anyone without a mother before, could not imagine how to grow up without a mom. The world had tilted, and I had no idea what else might happen that could be even more terrible.

Nothing in my father's life to this point had prepared him to be a single parent. In fact, just the opposite. He had been raised in modest circumstances during the Depression, an average student, the awkward older brother of a star athlete. His parents never owned a home. He never had a bicycle. He worked to pay his own way through college, including a stint as a school bus driver. Coming of age and marrying in the 1950s, his role as breadwinner defined his identity. Around the house he did traditional men's tasks like cutting grass and trimming bushes. My mom cooked, cleaned, and tended the children. They had met while she was still in high school as my dad attended the local Catholic men's college with her brothers. Her parents had a beer tap in the basement, so their house was the social hangout. Curled black-and-white snapshots of the time show men in white shirts, skinny ties, and dark trousers, and women wearing slim dresses, large clip earrings, and dark lipstick, all of them laughing or smiling with cigarettes held between two fingers off to the side and beers clasped in front.

School pictures of my dark-haired, dark-eyed mom suggest a serious, brainy young woman pursuing her goal of becoming a nurse. She attended a local Catholic women's college, and they married after my dad's two years in the army. He began working for her father's company, which sold supplies and equipment to hair salons, known then as beauty shops. My older brother arrived nine months later. His babyhood was well documented in photos depicting my mom, still in her early twenties, first beaming as she clutched her precious bundle and then delighting in his milestones. She stopped working as a nurse sometime after Mike was born and fully embraced motherhood. Over the next five years, the photo archive hints at but does not explicitly convey the ensuing heartaches: a stillborn baby girl, a midterm miscarriage, and then the premature birth of my older sister, Kate. My mom's smile is tired but joyful as she cradles her tiny daughter, home from the hospital two months later. It took much longer to discover that Kate had been permanently blinded by receiving too much oxygen in the incubator.

An obstetrician finally diagnosed my mom with an "incompetent cervix," meaning it could not hold a baby to full term, so during her next pregnancy, with me, it was stitched closed, and I was delivered via a scheduled cesarean section with no complications. Two years later, the same protocol was followed for my younger brother, but in the process my mom nearly died of a hemorrhage. Even with the challenges and heartbreaks of her childbearing, the photo record depicts her continued smiles around the backyard plastic pool, on picnics, surrounded by paper and bows on Christmas morning, clasping hands with my sister and me at the beach, and later holding Tim, seemingly content with each moment and welcoming each new stage as it came.

Nurturing Kate's needs wove naturally into my mom's life. She made sure that Kate participated in ordinary activities like swimming or the sandbox and guided her in how to safely get around the house and yard. After Kate started school, my mom not only learned to read braille but also earned certification as a transcriptionist so that she could actively help Kate learn to read and write, which were areas of struggle for her.

As the third child in the family, I always paid careful attention to what my older brother and sister were doing. By age four, I could not wait to go to school "like Mike and Kate." When I turned five in August, kindergarten could not start soon enough. Back then it was only half-day. The first morning, my mom and Tim dropped me off, with the plan that I would take the bus home at noon and then both to and from school each day after that. We parked on the street at Mt. Airy Elementary, a public school just up the road a short distance from our parish, and walked together to the playground on the right side of the wide one-story red brick building.

A woman standing at the entrance with a clipboard checked her list and pointed us to the first classroom just inside the door. My whole being buzzed with excitement and a tiny bit of fear as we said hello to my teacher, but I waved goodbye without looking back. Three hours later, walking in line onto the playground at dismissal, ready to conquer the bus-ride adventure, I spied Mom and Tim standing off to the side, scanning the stream of faces.

Stopping in my tracks, I wailed, "Why are you here? I want to ride the bus!"

"We were just at the grocery and thought we'd swing by," Mom said.

Tim stepped closer and started to tell me something, but I ignored him and scowled up at my mom, arms rigid at my sides.

"You really want to ride the bus?" she asked, tilting her head to one side and regarding me with a small curve to her lips.

"Yes!"

"Okay," she said, "we'll see you at home."

Such independence would prove to be both a strength and a burden in my life after Mom's death, but on this day, I was still an ordinary girl tussling with her mother.

Chapter Two

The house on Raeburn Drive where we lived when my childhood upended was itself a reversal, with the living room and family room on the second floor. I heard my dad say more than once that Mom "fell in love" with this house so they splurged and bought it. Coming up the hill into the subdivision, you couldn't miss it rising majestically on the corner of the main drive and a side street, in varied shades of brown brick with pillars painted dark brown extending its full two-story height. Though we normally went in and out through the garage, even as a child I appreciated the elegance of stepping into the spacious foyer from the front entrance in the center. The spiraling wood staircase straight ahead, the steps and railing stained dark like the floor, and the spindles painted white immediately drew the eye upward, and I imagined that this graceful view attracted my mom so strongly to the house.

Within weeks of Mom's death, Mrs. Noble came first in our series of live-in housekeepers. Plump and round, with graying red hair, she wore light blue polyester dresses almost like a nurse. Her white stockings swished when she walked, and she reeked of a sickly-sweet floral perfume that remains my strongest association of her.

"You must put on a jacket if you want to go outside," Mrs. Noble was saying wearily to Tim as I entered the kitchen one late afternoon.

This room occupied the lower right side of the house, a literal and symbolic cornerstone of our family that became alien territory without Mom. In daily life, entry to the kitchen from the front hall meant passing through the utility room, an oddity in childhood that now makes sense as it housed the water heater, furnace, washer, dryer, and stationary tub, as well as an ancient extra refrigerator that smelled funny inside, and a wall of cupboards that held coats, boots, and mittens along with shelves for toys and games. The house was built into a hill, my dad would explain, so we had a utility room instead of a basement. Brown paneling halfway up the wall defined the kitchen eating nook in the front corner with vinyl wallpaper above, a plaid pattern in olive green, orange, and white. A door to the outside led to the side yard.

Tim stood next to the table in a short-sleeved T-shirt, his back to the open outside door. His insistent refusal grabbed my attention, so I joined the fray.

"It's plenty warm out! He doesn't need a coat if he doesn't want one," I said defiantly from the utility room entry.

"Your father would not approve." She sighed, holding out the jacket.

"*I'm going!*" Tim shouted. His mouth formed a big O, and his face turned scarlet, tears spilling down his cheeks. He turned toward the exit and vented his frustration with a two-handed slam, shattering the bottom pane of the storm door. Shards went flying, and his rage turned to high-pitched screams of panic as Mrs. Noble stepped toward him.

"Stand still! Let me lift you over the broken glass!"

The scene unfolded in slow motion as blood dropped silently

to the floor like bright red dimes, and Tim cried harder. With a whooshing exhale, Mrs. Noble plopped into one of the chairs and pulled Tim to her lap. She grabbed a towel from the counter and pressed it to his forearm where a ribbon of blood was running down. Then she set him in the chair and moved to phone our across-the-street neighbor, Mrs. Rost, a nurse, who came over right away with first aid supplies. By then Tim's sobs had become hiccups, and I helped hold the towel while Mrs. Noble swept up the glass.

After a quick assessment, Mrs. Rost said, "It's just a small puncture. No stitches needed. A corner of glass probably landed there and then bounced right off."

As she finished wrapping Tim's arm with gauze, my dad walked in. Unspoken questions about what Dad would say when he got home already simmered among us, but he took it in stride, glad that Tim was okay, unperturbed about the broken glass, and appreciative of Mrs. Rost.

Now that Mrs. Noble lived with us, a stranger sat in my mom's chair during meals. Stilted conversation alternated with awkward silence over a constant tremor of tension. Though never articulated, inside I felt the searing juxtaposition of our new reality with memories of my mom. The old life had flowed seamlessly. As Tim and I ran in and out from playing in the driveway or the utility room, my mom peeled potatoes at the sink, watching out the window for Kate's return from school. She would quickly dry her hands on a towel and dash out to meet Kate at the street. Tim and I stood by when Mom made chocolate pudding, eager to lick the spoon and scrape the saucepan after she poured the rich steaming liquid into individual bowls for that night's dessert.

After Mom died, such ordinariness became disjointed. When Mrs. Noble made macaroni and cheese, the noodles went cold in the colander before she got around to stirring in the packaged cheese sauce, and then it wouldn't melt. Some days when it was time to leave for school, the lunches were not made. Though respectful to her when my dad was around, on our own I often reacted to Mrs. Noble as I had the afternoon of the broken storm door, resisting direction, asserting my own way. She meant well, but I was not having it. Lacking words to express loss, in these early days I acted it out.

Later came Mrs. Rudolph, who was more easygoing but also more eccentric. It amused us that she called the refrigerator the "Frigidaire." However, she took liberties with the liquor cabinet (I learned years after) and did not last long in our employ. Around this same time, my dad made the painful decision to enroll Kate as a boarding student at the state school for the blind in Columbus, two hours away. He later said it was the hardest thing he ever did but felt it was necessary. No one could ever replace my mom's dedicated attention to Kate's social and educational needs, so a specialized institution would have to fill the gap. Now Kate traveled home every few weekends on the Greyhound bus. Naturally introverted, she accepted the arrangement stoically, and I think we were all growing accustomed to sudden changes.

Finally, in the only example of family decision-making that I recall in my entire growing up, as a group we agreed to dispense with housekeepers and manage on our own. The deliberation occurred around the kitchen table, the question raised by my dad, and no one hesitated to support the idea. By this time, a year or so after my mom's death, he was ready to take on some cooking, and he would hire someone to clean and do laundry. Mike could supervise after school most days. Our grandparents would help with casseroles and driving us to doctor appointments.

I felt relieved to eliminate strangers from our midst, willing to risk the unknowns of being a latchkey child. I sensed a fledgling teamwork among us, survivors taking tiny steps forward. At the same time, we took emotional cues from Dad, who guarded against pain by staying focused on practical matters. If household tasks were covered and school arrangements handled, we convinced ourselves, then all was well enough.

Chapter Three

Now school mornings began with my dad's footfalls coming up the wood stairs, the quiet opening of the bedroom I mostly occupied alone, and then his cheerful booming, "It's time to rise and shine!" I'd groan and sit up, so he knew I'd get up. The night before, I had draped my school clothes over the desk chair, so the required red-and-green plaid uniform jumper, short-sleeved white blouse with pointed collar, red cardigan, and red knee socks awaited me, with oxford shoes beneath the chair. Now nine and in the fourth grade, I prized order and organization. My canvas tote bag leaned against the desk with its contents arranged in graduating order of size. Math, social studies, science, spelling, and language arts assignments were completed and filed in the proper pocket folders. My zippered case of pencils and pens was tucked neatly alongside the textbooks, spiral notebooks, and folders.

Standing before the wide dresser with its attached mirror, I picked up my brush and pulled it through my thick brown hair now below my shoulders. Before my mom died, my hair was always cut short in a pixie. She had said I could have my much-coveted long hair when I was old enough to care for it myself. In her absence, my hair had grown out seemingly without anyone's notice. It usually took multiple tries to get my ponytail in place at the back of my head, off my neck, smooth and firm but not too tight. Then I would make my bed and grab my book bag.

The expressive young girl I had been, the girl with a mom, would have dashed downstairs demanding a frozen waffle, but circumstances had sculpted a mature, capable outer persona that masked inner anxiety. As Responsible Girl on school mornings, I first checked on Tim before proceeding to breakfast. He might be up, his hair standing on end from sleep, but not all the way dressed. He could be leaning on the side of his bed hunched over a workbook, pencil in hand, doing forgotten homework.

"Hurry up," I admonished, exasperated.

Responsible Girl would gather up any books and folders that were scattered on the floor and stuff them in his bag, then go into the bathroom for a comb and a cup of water. Intent on her task, she'd startle when Dad called up the stairs, "What are you two doing? Come down and eat, or we'll be late!"

"Coming!"

Tim's hair tamed, the cup and comb back on the sink, we picked up our bags.

At school, I was one of the smart kids who genuinely enjoyed learning, and the classroom provided a level playing field where being motherless seldom came up, unlike lunchtime. Seated at the long cafeteria table surrounded by normal children with mothers, I so envied the way they eagerly opened their brown paper bags, each of them wondering what kind of sandwich his or her mom had made that morning. From third grade on, I always knew what was in my lunch, because I had made it myself. A sandwich, sometimes peanut butter and jelly but often bologna with yellow mustard, accompanied by Fritos or potato chips, a Hostess Fruit Pie or Ho Ho, or cookies.

The Art of Reassembly

My dad made the lunches for a short time after we discontinued housekeepers. He spread the peanut butter thickly on the bread and dolloped generous blobs of grape jelly directly on it before topping it with the other slice of bread. The proper method—the way Mom had done it—was to apply peanut butter to one slice, jelly to the other, and then put them together. I want to say that I never complained about his sandwiches, but prior to morphing into Responsible Girl, I probably did exclaim freely, "You put way too much peanut butter and jelly on the bread! I can't eat it!" A mom takes this sort of thing in stride, but perhaps my dad did not, or maybe he merely chose to simplify his own routine.

Either way, one morning when we entered the kitchen before school, he said, "From now on, you're going to make your own lunches." Though said without any rancor, his tone held a firmness that silenced any objection or plea that might have arisen. Standing straight, like a soldier, I blinked back tears and stepped to the counter where he had laid out bread, a knife, and jars.

In the late afternoon upstairs in the TV room, I often curled in the corner of the couch with a library book, immersed in the imaginary world where Ginnie's mom served homemade chocolate cake and cold milk after school and all loose ends tied up neatly at the end of twelve chapters. Besides the Ginnie and Geneva series and other books about girls my age, I also loved mysteries, and I read a lot of biographies, from presidents and first ladies to Helen Keller and Elizabeth Blackwell.

With my mom's tutelage, I had obtained my first library card the year before she died. We had sat together at the kitchen table as I labored to write my name in cursive as required by the library. She had leaned back in her chair, a cigarette perched between the first two fingers of her left hand, while, next to her, my small figure hunched over the paper. My fingers had gripped the pen in my attempts to mimic the letters she had written out as a model.

"It doesn't look right!" I had moaned in frustration because my efforts wandered down hill or spread too wide.

"That one looks better. Do you want to keep trying?" Mom had asked, sighing.

Persevering through my tears, I finally achieved sufficient competence to pass muster, and on a summer evening after dinner, we drove to the library. Mom filled out the basic information and passed the green card to me. I signed it and then marched to the desk, beaming. Mom stood well behind me as I reached up to hand the application to the librarian, who smiled encouragement. That night I checked out two books on a temporary card and walked to the car feeling several inches taller and much more grown-up. The real library card would be sent in the mail.

After Mom died, our neighbor, Mrs. Newman, took us to the library as part of our carpool arrangement. My dad drove in the morning, and she picked us up. My mom had first walked me up the street to the Newmans' to play one afternoon when I was about four. Leaving our house via the kitchen door, we had crossed the main road of the subdivision, turned left, and continued up the hill past five or six houses. Susan was a year older and Lizzy two years younger, and they became my first friends, especially Susan. After this initial visit, my mom would escort me across the street, and I'd walk the rest of the way by myself to play at their house. After I turned five, my mom let me cross by myself. Heart pounding, I would look both ways multiple times, watching carefully for the occasional car that might pass, then step off the curb, exhaling in relieved excitement as I made it safely to the other side.

From the start, I took a shine to Mrs. Newman. She and her husband owned a motel and restaurant where she worked on the weekends, and seeing her leave sometimes, all dressed up, I was entranced by her high heels, narrow skirts and dresses made of shimmery fabrics, dramatic eye makeup, and upswept frosted blond hair.

When I arrived at her car at the end of the school day, she would ask, "How was your day, Peg?" in a kind voice that welcomed whatever I wanted to share without prying. Though I never confided anything of substance, her practical acts of nurturing salved hidden wounds. At the beginning of the school year, she took us along to buy notebooks, folders, loose-leaf paper, pencils, and pens, and our library excursions took place every three or four weeks.

We visited a different branch than the one where my mom had taken us. It was a modern structure, almost pyramid-shaped, with a ramp walkway that went straight and then angled right to the glass doors to the library itself. You could also just walk up three steps to the doors, but I liked the ramp. Heading directly to the desk, I deposited my already-read books and strode over to the juvenile fiction section, immediately delving into possibilities. I chose decisively, realizing that our time there was finite.

After school, if I went to the Newmans' house to play, I always knew to return home at the long-established five-thirty deadline. Mrs. Newman would call down to the basement, "Peg, it's getting to be time." Susan could be bossy, and she and Lizzy often quarreled, so sometimes I was relieved to go. But more often, I said goodbye and thank you with a smile that hid a reluctance to leave. Trepidation grew as I walked slowly down the hill. Passing our next-door neighbor's and rounding the slight curve, would I see lights shining through the wide triple window over our kitchen sink?

Illumination meant Dad was home and fixing dinner. Stepping through the kitchen door, I would feel myself drawn into a family story that was my own, however flawed or different from my friends. I might set the table or sit down and listen while Dad and Mike talked and Dad finished cooking. Then we would call Tim and sit down to whatever Dad had thrown together. It might be tuna noodle casserole from Grandma, Hamburger Helper in the skillet, hot dogs and baked beans, pancakes and sausage, or grilled cheese sandwiches. Afterward, we cleared the table, Mike loaded the dishwasher, and then we adjourned to our rooms for homework.

Darkness behind the windows when I returned from the Newmans' would crush my hopes for a cheerful homecoming, and profound sadness particular to feeling motherless would envelop me like a fog. Inside, the empty feeling of falling through space opened an internal chasm, and I tensed my body against imminent tears, attempting to quell the accompanying anxiety. Stomach clenched, I'd force myself over the threshold into the desolate kitchen, flicking the light switch to the right of the door to dispel some of the gloom before trudging upstairs to join Mike and Tim. Dad would arrive soon, but it didn't matter. A pall had been cast.

Grandma Wimberg, my mom's mom, and I sat in the gold vinyl chairs at her speckled white Formica kitchen table next to the window of their second-floor apartment. The duplex, red brick on the bottom with white siding on top, perched on a hill. Though the view overlooked the yard below and a busy street beyond, our eyes focused directly in front of us on the seven piles of cards laid out in alternating red-and-black sequence on the table. She was teaching me solitaire.

A petite woman with an oval face framed by a cap of gray hair and set off by round glasses, her fingernails were painted red, though often chipped. She dressed in skirts and blouses or dresses, and she wore support stockings with her pumps. Around the apartment, she donned a large cotton print apron that went over her head and tied on the sides to protect her clothing while cooking or doing other tasks. Though more soft-spoken than gregarious, she had a ready laugh.

As I turned over sets of three cards from the remaining deck, Grandma offered subtle clues about possible plays. When the ace or jack that I needed to open up the rest of the game remained unavailable, sometimes I turned over hidden cards just to have the satisfaction of matching the red and black in numerical order and building four neat piles, one for each suit, a "win." Sitting next to me, Grandma just chuckled indulgently and sipped her coffee. Then she would shuffle the cards so I could play again if I wanted.

Her daily rosary took priority, always. I knew at some point she would withdraw to her room with her rosary beads and small black prayer book containing scripture verses, prayers, and colored pictures of the joyful, sorrowful, and glorious mysteries, events in the life of Mary and Jesus to be recollected with that day's rosary recitation. A hush descended on the apartment as she knelt by the bed, lips moving and eyes often closed. I disliked this interruption to our activity but understood that it mattered to her. Sometimes before or after these prayer sessions, I asked questions, and she explained the order of prayers around the beads.

Responsible Girl's presence was not required at Grandma's, where we drank Coke out of light-green eight-ounce glass bottles and slept on the pullout couch in the TV room. Sunday mornings meant mass at their parish with eggs, bacon, and coffee cake after. Evenings, Grandpa listened to baseball games on the radio. Sometimes I accompanied Grandma to the grocery store or watched her fold laundry. Throughout, we talked about everyday things like errands she needed to run or friends who were coming to visit, a kind of normalcy I craved, and I sometimes unburdened myself of things I could say to no one else.

"Mike got really bad grades on his report card, and Dad pounded his fist on the kitchen counter and yelled so loud I heard it upstairs. I hate when he does that," I said, blinking back tears. "Then," I continued, sniffing, "Tim left his bike in the driveway, and Dad grounded him for a week."

Listening, her lips tightened, giving her face a pained look as she cast her gaze downward, sighing and shaking her head slightly, hand on her cheek, but she just allowed my words to be there, without criticizing my dad or offering false comfort. After a minute, she might lean in to give me a quick hug, or we might move on to another topic.

Too soon Sunday evening would arrive, and it was time to leave. The drive across town in the setting sun induced melancholy as the need to activate Responsible Girl returned. Experience had taught me to curate what I shared with Dad about activities at Grandma's. He did not like hearing about us being "spoiled" by staying up late or indulging in sweets. Once he warned that he would not let us go there anymore, which I assumed was an idle threat but did not want to find out. Clearly there were underlying tensions between my dad and his in-laws, but their exact nature went beyond my ability or desire to understand.

On weekends that we stayed at home, Saturday nights developed a contrasting routine with Responsible Girl at the helm. Dad always went out, dressed in a sport jacket and tie and smelling of aftershave, to parties, restaurants, or events. We never knew the specifics and did not much care, though on one rare occasion, a group of couples that included a date for him met up at our house before attending a charity function.

"I'll see you in the morning," he'd say, leaning to kiss my cheek as I hugged him briefly around the waist, inhaling the scent of his Old Spice aftershave. "Mike will fix dinner."

"Bye," I said, clinging for a brief second.

The Art of Reassembly

The door to the garage slammed lightly behind him, and moments later the Buick's engine revved. We never tattled on each other, so no one let on to Dad that Mike often took off early for his evening, leaving dinner to Responsible Girl. A little later she would preheat the oven to four hundred degrees for the chicken potpies. She removed two of them from the freezer compartment at the top of the refrigerator (three if Kate was home), opened the packages, cut the required one-inch slit in the top crust, placed them on a baking sheet, and set the timer for forty-five minutes.

It was much quieter without Mike's smart-aleck humor, and though we were never afraid on our own, sometimes I missed the energy of his presence on these nights. More often though, Responsible Girl enjoyed being capable and in control. Shortly before the timer beeped, she set the table and called Tim in from the driveway. Carefully removing the hot pan from the oven with potholders, she transferred each bubbling potpie to a plate. After we ate and threw the little tins in the trash, she put the plates in the dishwasher, washed the baking sheet, and wiped the counters. Often, she swept the floor, like Laura in the Little House books, imagining herself in the story with a mother assigning this chore.

After playing some more, we took our baths and dressed in pajamas and robes. Continuing as Responsible Girl, I began the popcorn ritual, measuring corn and oil, pouring both into the small bowl space at the center of the Hamilton Beach popper before placing the clear yellow plastic cover over it and plugging it in. I loved watching the oil begin to bubble around the kernels as it heated and seeing the kernels bulge as the heat built up, followed by the light *plink, plink* sound as they started to pop, which built to a pounding before slowing again. Then I unplugged the popper, gripped the side handles of both top and bottom, and flipped the appliance over, converting the plastic top to a handy serving bowl. Tim had poured Coke over ice in the tall green-hued glasses. Upstairs, we settled onto the couch to munch the hot salty popcorn and watch *Mary Tyler Moore*, *Bob Newhart*, and *The Carol Burnett Show*.

I had learned the difficulty of washing oil from the plastic dome top that became the serving bowl, so during a commercial after we had eaten our fill, I ran down to the kitchen, dumped the unpopped kernels in the trash, squirted Ivory liquid dish soap into the bowl, and ran hot water. At ten o'clock, after *Carol Burnett* ended, I put the glasses in the dishwasher, washed and dried the popcorn popper, and returned it to the lower cabinet. I made sure Tim brushed his teeth, brushed my own, and then we both went to bed. To us, this was just a normal way to be at home.

On a Sunday afternoon, there were no sweeter words to hear Dad call up the stairs than "Anybody want to take a ride out to see the Bowmans?"

"*Yes!*"

Dear friends of my parents, Jim and Rebecca and their three children had been part of our lives for as long as I could remember. We dropped what we were doing and got in the car, no need to change clothes or clean up. The Bowmans' house meant laughter and play, snacks and dinner, and often staying up late. They provided a refuge for my dad as my grandma did for me, and when he relaxed, I could too. We sought solace where we could, but we never spoke of our pain.

Chapter Four

On a balmy late afternoon in the spring of 1974, Dad summoned us to the kitchen as soon as he returned from work, which was unusual. Mike, Tim, and I took our seats at the table, wondering what was going on as he stood next to the counter still in his work attire. His hazel eyes were bright, and his cheeks held a rosy glow, beaming even. A frisson of expectancy stirred as Dad regarded us with a small smile and then cleared his throat before speaking.

"I have news . . . I'm getting remarried," he announced, sounding pleased but also amazed, as though he couldn't quite believe it himself.

After a brief silence, Mike said, "That's great!" in an unfamiliar, hearty voice, followed by my tentative query, "To Miss Cook?"

"Yes," he replied.

"When?"

"Probably in November," Dad said.

Although Miss Cook had been among the group that appeared at our house the previous fall, I had attached no significance to her presence at the time. Between that introduction and the engagement announcement, we had had a few visits to her apartment with Dad on Christmas and Easter afternoons and perhaps one or two other times. Later my dad jovially referred to the year or so of their courtship as "the campaign." Clearly, he had strategized—successfully it turned out—to clinch their couple relationship before bringing his four children into the mix. Dad began actively seeking a new wife two years after my mom's death, and people fixed him up with lots of different women (all those Saturday nights we were home eating potpies and popcorn). He was introduced to Miss Cook through their mutual friend, Jim Bowman. Though initially put off by her status as a former nun, he allowed Mr. Bowman to convince him to at least meet her.

The engagement news heralded a major shift in our family, but sitting in the kitchen that day, there wasn't a whole lot else to say and nothing for us to do about it, so we returned to our after-school pursuits, outwardly business as usual. Inside, my whole being hummed with curiosity about what this might mean. I was going on eleven, and the idea of a stepmother preoccupied my thoughts like a newfound crush. Undaunted by evil stepmothers in literature, I instead fantasized about school lunches being made by a mother figure who greeted us after school with freshly baked cookies and created real home-cooked meals so the kitchen would always be warm and bright. Like the von Trapp family in my favorite movie, *The Sound of Music*, an attractive former nun would marry the sad, stern widower and bring music back into the lives of the motherless children.

Miss Cook wasn't quite elegant like Mrs. Newman, but she dressed stylishly and wore makeup with bright lipstick. I allowed unspoken hope that Responsible Girl could be left behind after the wedding. The first time we saw her following the engagement, Miss Cook said that we could call her "Aggie," though most adults called her just "Ag." During her fifteen years as a religious sister, Aggie had been a high school teacher and a college admissions director. She had left her religious community about a year before meeting my dad, and at the time of their marriage, she worked downtown for the phone company in human resources.

About sixty guests celebrated the wedding, including my mom's family, at an afternoon affair that was too simple for my eleven-year-old taste. Aggie wore an ankle-length plain white knit dress, belted at the waist, and my dad a brown suit. Though I would have preferred more traditional finery, the biggest letdown was the tiered trays of individual petits fours rather than an actual wedding cake. Aggie smiled when I expressed dismay on this matter. "At our age, we don't need a fancy wedding." Still, I had fun at the event running around with my new same-age cousin, Colleen, the daughter of Aggie's older sister.

Aggie moved in right after the wedding, and the novelty of it captivated me. As if I had drawn in a big breath, I held myself in suspension, waiting and watching to see what would happen. Quickly we learned that Aggie was highly organized in all aspects of living. Immediately she began the practice of planning a weekly menu so that she could grocery shop once and have all the necessary ingredients on hand. She put a notepad by the refrigerator for us to write down things we needed from the store. She established six fifteen as the official dinnertime. Sometimes Responsible Girl's services were required to meet this schedule. We all really liked a recipe she found in a *Better Homes & Gardens* magazine involving cream-of-mushroom-soup mixture poured over chicken breasts and baked in a Pyrex casserole dish, accompanied by Rice-A-Roni. Aggie wrote a note listing what to do and when and reviewed it with me the night before. I cheerfully executed these tasks when required; they weren't difficult and didn't take long. Encouraged by my dad, Aggie also found it practical to have us continue making our own lunches since she had to get herself off to work in the morning. Responsible Girl said nothing, of course, and continued her morning routine as usual.

Soon after her arrival, Aggie undertook to clean out the linen cupboard, which was a set of shelves behind sliding wood doors in the short entry hall to the master bedroom. Pulling out a stack of white towels from the top left, she turned to place them in my arms and said, "Go hang these in the hall bathroom," meaning the one just outside my room that was used by family, primarily my siblings and me, and visitors. My mom had called these "the good towels" when she put them out only for infrequent special occasions. They were thick and fluffy with her initials embroidered in burgundy. To my young mind, that the largest initial for the last name strangely appeared in the center of the monogram only added to their mystique. Even though the guests surely would not be showering, the bath towels were hung on the wall rack and the hand towels placed by the sink.

I started to say to my new stepmother, "Those are the good . . ." but her blue eyes looked cool and hard like marbles above her wide smile, and a quivery sensation I didn't understand closed my throat against further words.

"Might as well get use out of them," Aggie said, chipper. "No sense sitting on the shelf."

Something felt wrong, but instinct fixed a neutral expression on my face, and Responsible Girl carried out her instructions.

Just weeks after the wedding, for the first time in years, we hosted Thanksgiving at our house, for my dad's parents and Aggie's sister and her two teenaged daughters. The night before, when I heard Aggie moving around in the dining room, which opened off the front hall, I descended the spiral stairs slowly, trying to peek in, and then stood quietly just outside the light splashing from the usually dark dining room. Aggie had changed from her work pantsuit to jeans and a ribbed turtleneck and knelt before the open buffet compartments, considering. When she glanced up, her eyes were soft. I inched closer and stood in the doorway for a beat until curiosity overcame inhibition.

"What are you doing?"

"Setting the table for tomorrow night. I'll need to focus on the meal in the morning, so I want to get this out of the way."

"Oh."

"Would you like to help?"

"Okay," I replied, kneeling beside her on the olive-green carpet.

We unearthed my mom's china, the creamy plates round and flat with a gold-accented deep-pink rose at the center and a thin gold rim. I had not seen them in a long time, but I remembered how much I loved that pink rose.

"These are so pretty," I said softly, but Aggie had moved on to the cordovan-stained wood chest containing my mom's sterling flatware, thick with embossed flowers. Though her demeanor was businesslike, she moved carefully, her gestures almost reverent in her handling of each item. Silently, I soaked it all up like a sponge as Aggie began a running commentary, now unpacking items they had just received for their wedding.

"This is our new breadbasket," she said, holding up a silver mesh oval and then passing it to me. "Put that on the table, please."

Then she turned to a large box full of packing peanuts and pulled out a round sterling pan with several parts. "We'll use this chafing dish for the mashed potatoes." She set that on the buffet.

"My friends Jane and Dick O'Toole gave us these silver wine goblets," she said, beaming as she held them out for me to admire their engraved names and wedding date on each.

Aggie had already covered the table with a white cloth embroidered with colorful flowers. Picking the top napkin off the stack before her, she said, "These go on the left side of the plate. Fold them this way, with the open side facing right, toward the plate, so it unfolds properly when picked up."

I had been too young to ever assist with these fine items when my mom was alive, so such niceties were all brand-new to me. Fascinated, I practiced napkin folding under Aggie's watchful eye and then moved around the table placing each one, just so. Aggie followed with dinner plates, positioning them so the rose was upright, then modeled how to set the fork just beside the napkin to the left of the plate and knife and spoon on the right, and to line them up straight across the bottom, followed by the bread plates to the left, with individual butter knives laid across the top. Lastly, we placed the crystal water goblets and wine glasses etched with twisting vines that were from my mom—water to the left of the knife tip, wine on the right and down a little lower.

Everything arranged, we stepped back to appreciate our sparkling tableau.

"It looks nice, don't you think?" Aggie said.

"Yes, it's beautiful!" Suddenly shy, I added, "Well, goodnight, Aggie."

"Goodnight. Thanks for your help."

"You're welcome. It was fun."

I went up to bed in a state of wonder about the unprecedented evening. Is this what it felt like to have a mother? Could I trust my feelings? Could I trust Aggie? It was all so intriguing. Only a few blurry photos, taken the next day with a Kodak Instamatic camera, commemorate this inaugural family holiday. Their poor quality did not dim the recent bride's beaming expression as she posed beside the gleaming table, wearing a long wraparound jumper in a bright patchwork pattern with a red turtleneck underneath. There is a shot of the table by itself from a different angle along with another where a finger obstructs most of the view. I am not pictured.

The Art of Reassembly

That first Christmas after my dad's remarriage, Aggie switched up all our past customs. Where before we went to our mom's extended family on Christmas Eve, had "Santa" on Christmas morning at home, and then dinner at my dad's parents on Christmas Day, Aggie's bold new plan called for Christmas Eve at home with just us, and a simple meal followed by leisurely opening of presents together rather than a mad dash on Christmas morning. Grandma and Grandpa Morse would then come to our house for a festive dinner as they had on Thanksgiving. I accepted the change as a matter of course. Still holding my breath as our new life continued to reveal itself, I was also used to having adults make plans without consulting the kids.

That Christmas Eve may have been the longest interval I had ever spent in our unusual upstairs living room. Several weeks earlier, Aggie had asked each of us for a list of gift suggestions, and she shopped downtown on her lunch hours. On Christmas Eve, we ate bowls of chili in the kitchen before convening in the high-ceilinged room, the mood a combination of eager and awkward, where Aggie passed out a present to each person to take turns, one at a time, opening them. This went on for several rounds, punctuated with laughter and oohs and aahs as the paper was torn away and the contents were revealed. I worried that Christmas morning would feel empty afterward, but the newness of it all held me rapt.

The annual Cook family Christmas party was added to our holiday repertoire, on one of the nights before New Year's. Aggie's three sisters and her brother along with their families gathered at rotating houses for a meal and to exchange group gifts, like board games, among the family units. Aggie was the youngest in her family, so most of her nieces and nephews were grown, but there were a couple around my age to pal around with. The aunts and uncles all welcomed us warmly, and I felt at ease in their company. A shiny new story was taking shape around us, it seemed.

Chapter Five

It strikes me that I do not recall how or when I learned that we would be moving across town to a new house and, further, that this news did not upset me. Dad said they wanted us to start fresh in a new home. I felt excited; it seemed like an adventure I had read about in a library book, the plot building toward the happy ending now. Privately I thought the new house seemed a bit of a comedown. Built in the colonial revival style, it was red brick, rectangular, and symmetrical, with a steeply pitched slate roof. The front hall was just a small area inside the front door, with a coat closet across and an ordinary carpeted staircase going up straight ahead. The living room was on the right and the dining room on the left, connected along the back by the kitchen and adjacent breakfast room. I liked that the dining room had a bay window and a built-in corner cabinet where Aggie eventually placed the china and crystal. The rooms seemed boxy and cramped compared to Raeburn, the effect of lower ceilings. The house did have a basement that Aggie and Dad planned to remodel into a family room.

Aggie worked with a decorator to transform the main rooms prior to our move. In the kitchen, new cabinetry and countertops, fresh wallpaper, and new appliances were installed, including the newfangled microwave as the top oven. The living and dining rooms, downstairs and upstairs halls, and master bedroom had new wallpaper and wall-to-wall carpet in a peachy-orange and light-green color scheme that sounds dreadful but was actually attractive, though a bit shocking in comparison to the understated blues at Raeburn. Aggie kept most of the furniture, reupholstered to match the new decor, creating a colorful backdrop for our new story.

I didn't fully comprehend what moving meant until the event was upon me. At school on the very last day, I received gifts and notes from my teachers and friends, and there was a celebration in the afternoon with cake. Then finally the enormity of what was happening set in, and at home that evening, I sobbed in my room as I reread the cards. The ground was shifting under my feet, and I didn't know what to grab for stability. I had been going to school with the same kids since kindergarten, but now I'd become a "new kid." I had a close circle of girlfriends and a best friend named Susan, relationships that were just beginning to mature. It was the start of Presidents' Day weekend. Tim and I went to stay over at Aunt Connie and Uncle Jack's with Colleen. She and I were about to become classmates.

We began at our new school the following Tuesday. Keeping with our pattern of abrupt change, that morning Dad took Tim and me to the school for the first time. We parked next to the box-like gray concrete building at the top of a hill. On the way in, I felt sick to my stomach. Of course, the girls milling about the playground wore black-and-white saddle shoes and ski jackets while, in the fashion of my prior school, I had oxfords and a long brown wool coat trimmed with brocade, a garment that until that moment I had loved dearly. Now I felt it as a screaming symbol of difference that made me stand out when all I wanted to do was blend in, or better yet to sink into the floor or run away as fast as I could. Instead, I was rather fixed in place. My arms woodenly by my side and facing forward, unseeing, I followed my dad up the stairs to the office and talked with the principal. My face felt frozen, and I could hardly speak to answer his simple, friendly questions because my lips were trembling. I was on the brink of tears. Although Colleen shepherded me through the day, which passed in a blur, I felt like I had landed in a foreign country.

Grandma and Grandpa Wimberg lived only a mile or so from our new house on Principio Avenue and just a few blocks from my new school, part of the parish where we had often attended mass with them, all in an easily walkable neighborhood. I could visit them whenever I wanted. I had looked forward to that proximity, and it was fun at first. A few weeks after the move, on a Saturday, I felt free to stop in with a new friend, Elaine, to use the phone and check in with our families about our plan for the afternoon after attending a sports event at school. With her usual ease and cheer, Grandma made us ham salad sandwiches and asked inter-ested questions.

A few months later, inexplicably, her face remained unexpres-sive as we sat at the kitchen table like strangers when I stopped by one afternoon after school.

"I'm going to play on the softball team," I attempted. "Practice starts next week."

"Oh, that's nice," she replied, her voice sounding flat as she gazed out the window rather than meeting my eyes.

The old grandma would have raised her eyebrows as an open-ing for the uncertainty in my tone, and I would have poured out my apprehensions. I didn't enjoy sports, but every single girl in the class seemed to participate on teams. She would have heard my concern but offered a philosophical reassurance. Instead, we sat in awkward silence.

I tried again. "Aggie sent in an application for the swim club. She said we'll probably be on the waiting list this summer. I wish we'd get in sooner."

"Is that right?"

I finally stopped going after one or two more tries. With rare openness, I let tears spill out with Dad and Aggie when I returned home from a grim encounter. They displayed unusual empathy in return, saying it wasn't my fault and suggesting I need not go anymore if I didn't want to. Even as a sixth grader, intuitively I grasped that things had changed for Grandma too. As I grew older, I imagined the loss of her role in our lives following my dad's remarriage caused her to confront the death of her eldest daughter yet again, and I wished she would have shared her feelings with me.

We still saw Grandma and Grandpa and my aunt Jeanne at Christmas, but it was a separate, small group gathering, not the "real" holiday, almost like there had been a divorce. We were included in major occasions like my grandparents' fiftieth anniversary or my cousin's wedding, but, overall, we began living separate storylines. I was much too young to comprehend the origins or implications of this relational shift. Then, an engrossing new character propelled my narrative further in this alternate direction.

Chapter Six

On Easter afternoon, about three months following our move, as we sat around the table after brunch, an upbeat Dad glanced around and then announced, "We're going to have an addition to the family."

"A dog?" I blurted. But no, he meant a baby, due in late August.

Mark Edward Morse arrived in the early morning of September 1, 1975, at seven pounds, five ounces, and twenty-one inches long. It was a cesarean birth, which at the time meant a hospital stay of eight days. The afternoon of their homecoming, Tim and I walked back from school together, coaching each other and resolving, "Just say how cute he is, no matter what he looks like!" We had little prior exposure to babies but had heard that newborns could have misshapen heads or red faces.

In fact, I exclaimed, "Oh, he looks so sweet!" in spontaneous, sincere amazement when I saw Mark for the first time, lying on his back in the porta-crib. He looked perfect and precious with even-toned light-pink skin, a symmetrically round face with cheeks that were full but not chubby, just the right amount of brown hair, neither bald nor bushy, and dark eyes.

The dining room served as baby central for the first few weeks.

The Art of Reassembly

The porta-crib stood against the wall to the right of the front bay window, and the table served as the dressing and changing area. As she did with everything, Aggie took an organized approach and was matter-of-fact and deliberate about Mark's care. I watched her bathe him for the first time in the kitchen. She narrated every step aloud, quoting instructions received at the hospital. After setting up all the necessary supplies, she laid him on a padded area of folded towels next to the sink, keeping him covered except for the area she was bathing so he didn't get cold. She wiped his eyes with a damp cotton ball, used a small washcloth to be sure water and suds got into the folds of his neck, and dipped a Q-tip in alcohol to clean the cord area. Mark was an easygoing baby who tolerated all of this without fussing, gazing at the light above the sink. I stood by, eagerly soaking it all in.

I never actually bathed him myself when he was tiny, but soon I learned to give him bottles. Every other day or so, Aggie boiled all the feeding paraphernalia, then poured formula into the bottles and put them in the refrigerator. She used the microwave to carefully heat them up before feeding. She demonstrated and explained how to fit the nipple into the top ring and screw it on the bottle and then how to sprinkle a little milk on my forearm to test the warmth. The usual feeding spot was in the living room, in the chair and ottoman by the bookshelf. After Mark drank about two ounces, it was time to try burping. Rather than putting him over her shoulder, Aggie espoused the less-common method of sitting the baby up in your lap, leaned a bit forward so that your hand under his chin with the towel to catch any spit-up also helped support him, and the other hand in back, partially in support but also patting his back to elicit the burp.

Mark was about eight weeks old the first time I babysat him on my own on a Saturday evening while Aggie and Dad went out to dinner with friends. By then rice cereal had been added to his nine-o'clock feeding. I followed what I had been shown and taught, getting the bottle heated and mixing the cereal, while Mark sat perched in his little baby seat. I had changed his diaper and dressed him in a sleeper already so that I could put him in the crib right after. With the lights dimmed as an encouragement toward sleep, I picked him up and sat with his head in the crook of my left arm and managed the feeding and bottle with my right. I remember feeling a little nervous at the weight of responsibility for this little person but, once into it, found it fun, like having a live doll.

I loved holding Mark. Evenings, I often walked around the living room with him on my shoulder after dinner while Aggie cleaned up the kitchen, lulling him to sleep if he was fussy. The baby smell and the weighted warmth of his little body against mine with his head snuggled up to my neck intoxicated me, an attraction made even more irresistible a few months later when he visibly responded to my presence, smiling in recognition and waving his arms and legs when I came in to pick him up out of the crib after a nap.

One Saturday afternoon while Mark was asleep upstairs in his crib, out of the blue as usual my dad and Aggie called Tim and me down to the living room for a startling conversation. Dad spoke for them both.

"Ag wants to adopt you kids. That way, she'll be your legal mother, so if anything ever happened to me, there would be no question of who would take care of you. She would be your mother, and you'd stay together."

Tim and I looked back at him without speaking.

She would adopt Kate, Tim, and me, but Mike did not qualify because he was already past age eighteen. The court system would process it, of course, and a social worker would be coming next week to talk to us and ask us if this was okay.

"So, you'll say yes, right?" His voice went higher, though it was not a question. We nodded, the expected response.

"Oh, something else—she'll explain that your birth certificate will be changed to say that Agnes Cook is your mother," Dad added smoothly, trying to sound casual.

Aggie was next to him on the couch, while Tim and I sat on the love seat to their right. She smiled wide, her eyes bright and her head leaning to one side. At twelve years old, I ignored the unease that surged through me. I could not face how much it bothered me to lose my mom's name on my birth document and that Mike was not included. His birth certificate would stay the same, and he would not be part of this new story. Clearly my dad and Aggie wanted the adoption, and the carrot they dangled, of having an actual mother again, if only on paper, seemed to fulfill my deepest desire. Having lost a parent to death already, the offer of firm protection should the unthinkable happen to my dad naturally touched a nerve.

"It's only a piece of paper. It really doesn't matter," Tim and I said to each other afterward when we were alone, rationalizing.

The adoption became final in December 1975, and the following spring on Mother's Day, the final piece was fitted into place. After church and breakfast, we presented Aggie with pots of geraniums for the garden beds flanking the front door. They were not a surprise gift, but she smiled and thanked us warmly.

"These are beautiful and will brighten up the yard so nicely."

Then, more softly and with uncharacteristic shyness, Aggie said, "I was wondering . . . I'd like to ask you . . . to call me Mom."

Tim and I said nothing at first, taken aback. Simultaneous disquiet and thrill shivered through me.

Gaining purpose, she continued. "I *am* legally your mother now, and Mark of course will call me that, and I think it would be nice for all of you to call me the same thing." She paused, then concluded with, "I would like it if you called me Mom."

Since that horrible November morning more than five years

earlier, we had only reluctantly spoken the word *Mom* when absolutely necessary, and then in a hushed tone of reverence. Could I call someone different by this sacred title? Allow it to become once again a common, everyday term? But Responsible Girl understood her duty.

Nodding, I said, "Oh, okay! Yes."

It was awkward at first to switch from calling her Aggie to Mom. I had to think about it. But it made things easier in some ways too, like out in public or at school where every other kid addressed their parents as Mom and Dad.

Later she gave me a small white box tied with a red ribbon. Inside, I discovered a tiny heart-shaped charm with a pink rose painted on it, hanging on a delicate gold chain. The accompanying gift note in her neat, even script explained that she had received the charm at her baptism, concluding with, "I'm so happy to have a daughter like you to give this to. Love, Mom."

Now I exhaled and stepped into my new role as Ag's Daughter. "Thank you! It's so pretty!" I said, smiling.

Chapter Seven

From my room I could hear Mom down the hall opening and closing drawers in her and Dad's bedroom as she put away clean laundry. In a surprisingly short time, it had become second nature to call her Mom instead of Aggie. Repeated daily use of the once-revered title had dulled the resonance of loss and created the image—internal and external—of being an ordinary teenager. Sighing in trepidation, I picked up the little flyer and went to her bedroom.

"Could you go over this with me now?" I spoke softly to Mom because Mark was asleep in the room across the hall. My face felt hot as I gestured with the folded paper that she had given me from a box of Tampax tampons the day before.

"Oh, okay, might as well," she said.

The practicalities of menstruation had arisen quite early in our relationship when my first period occurred just two months after the wedding, before we moved. My aunt had already given me some explanation, plus my sister is older than I am, so it wasn't totally unknown. I certainly wasn't going to consult my dad, so approaching Aggie that Friday evening in January seemed easy by comparison. She took the news in stride, found some pads somewhere, and all was fine. I felt kind of proud. The next day, the bleeding became heavy and clotted, and I curled up on my bed in mounting pain and fear of what my female future entailed. Half-consciously, I left my bedroom door wide open in hopes that Aggie would notice, and she did.

Peering in a bit later, she asked, "Oh, are you having cramps? Take some aspirin. I should have told you to do that," she said, sounding apologetic.

That was during sixth grade. At the time, Aggie had said I could use tampons when I got older, that they were a lot more convenient. Now, eighteen months later, living in a new neighborhood where we had just gained membership to the swim club, I wanted to hang out at the pool at every time of the month. Reading over the directions and studying the diagram in advance of this one-on-one lesson only heightened my anxiety. How in the world could this work? How embarrassing would this conversation be?

We moved to the tiny master bathroom, me standing in the doorway as she read aloud from the directions. Then she deftly pulled the string to open the individually wrapped tampon and explained how it pushed through the applicator. My eyes widened as she hoisted her right leg up on the closed toilet, a possible position offered in the package circular, and mimed its insertion.

"Remember to aim it toward your low back and push it in that direction. It's not straight upward. If you can stay relaxed, that will help," she said. Turning to face me again, she asked if I had any questions.

"No, I don't think so," I said, my mind spinning with the details but starting to calm as she continued to be matter-of-fact.

"I'd suggest putting some Vaseline on the outside of the applicator to help it go in more easily at first, till you get used to it. It's just going to take some practice," she concluded.

She handed me a turquoise-blue Tampax box of my own to put in the other bathroom.

"Thanks," I said.

It is common for motherless girls to feel deficient in female knowledge that one's peers seem to acquire effortlessly from their moms. As Ag's Daughter, I felt relief to have a mom shoring up this gap in my life, which she did quite effectively on many fronts. When I needed a dress for eighth-grade graduation or later for high school dances, she took me shopping at the mall. We would peruse the racks and select a few skirts or dresses before heading to the dressing room. If a different size or color or additional options altogether were required, Mom would run back and forth. Ever practical, she would also note multiple combinations that might be possible with my existing wardrobe.

Standing at the counter while our purchases were rung up, often the saleswoman would observe sweetly, "Your daughter looks just like you." Then Mom and I would exchange an amused glance, and she would reply only, "Thanks." Fully inhabiting the new story now, I didn't mind these remarks. Sometimes, such encounters even felt comforting.

The same warm feeling of "normal" washed over me when she and I attended a mother-daughter event at school or baked cookies at Christmas or continued our holiday table-setting tradition. Before long, she had taught me how to express sympathy at a funeral visitation, when to send a thank-you note and how to compose it, and, during high school when an older cousin got married, how to host a bridal shower. She modeled for me how to welcome a new neighbor and to support someone who is ill with meals or rides to the doctor. She even explained the intricacies of family trees so that I could define "once removed" cousins.

In subtle but important ways, I carried the weight of "not normal" in relation to Mom too. I loved walking to school, to piano lessons, and to friends' houses, and I relished having the library an easy bike ride away. Such freedom cut two ways though. When it was raining at three o'clock, Mom never came to pick us up from school. Mark took his nap then, so that was that. We always had to get our own rides on those occasions as well as to sports practices or social outings with friends. I took the city bus downtown to the dermatologist starting at age twelve, and she never once made our school lunches. Inwardly, I felt myself to be so much older than my classmates, as though I were an adult going to elementary school.

As Mark grew into a toddler, I looked forward to seeing him after school and often took him for walks in the stroller or played with him in the driveway, throwing balls or watching as he rode his little bike. It was so easy to embrace the new storyline with him, pure love right there in the moment, uncomplicated by wounds from a fractured past. When Mark was three, Dad bought his own business and began working much longer hours than before, including on weekends. This further bonded Mom, Mark, and me to a cozy trio, while Tim preferred to hang out with friends. As Mark grew, I regularly joined them for outings to state parks and historical sites and to the swim club. After I could drive, I took Mark on my own to play miniature golf or tennis.

It evolved then that Mom and I chatted about Mark a great deal. I might share my anecdotes of him along with observations about his strengths or interests or needs, though much more commonly I listened as she related what his preschool teacher said or how his soccer game went or the part he would have in the upcoming show or who had invited him to play or how much taller he was than at last year's checkup. I would nod and interject appropriate supportive comments when needed. She and I were united in mutual doting, and the recipient of our devotion looked to both of us for nurturing and guidance.

Particularly with Mark, being Ag's Daughter became a variation on Responsible Girl. From the time Mark was an infant until my dad bought his business, Mom and Dad went out together on Saturday nights, so I cared for Mark in addition to handling dinner, then put Mark to bed before we made the popcorn. On Wednesdays after school, Mom required Tim and me to alternate watching Mark while she did the weekly grocery shopping. We also babysat him while she had her hair done or went to the doctor.

I particularly resented the grocery duty after the comparative freedom of our latchkey days at Raeburn. I wanted to do my own thing after school. In my mind, a normal mother would simply take her toddler with her to the store. Why didn't she? Was it just inconvenient? Did she want a break? Or did it spring from an impulse to control or a drive for efficiency that was intrinsic to her personality? I did not dwell on her possible reasons, because Dad had tacitly handed her the reins to the household. We were expected to oblige her requests.

I went on to attend a Catholic girls' high school where I studied hard, served on the student council, and forged friendships, outwardly a successful teen but always wrestling with the sense of feeling too grown-up and wondering if others noticed that. After school one afternoon in the spring of my sophomore year, Mom knocked lightly before entering the room I shared with my sister, who continued to attend boarding school, and sat down on the end of Kate's twin bed with a small smile. Still wearing my black-watch-plaid uniform skirt and white blouse, I stood by my desk reviewing the evening's homework.

She allowed a brief silence before speaking. "I want to talk to you about something. You know that all my sisters have had breast cancer. I don't have it, but I'm getting closer to the ages they were when they were diagnosed with it, so this summer I'm going to have a double mastectomy as a preventive measure."

In her straightforward manner, she went on to explain how she'd have implants, but some tissue would remain because she'd keep her nipples, meaning a small chance of developing breast cancer would remain, but the risk would be much reduced if not fully eliminated.

"The surgery will be on June 12, and I'll be in the hospital for about a week. . . . I'd like you to take care of Mark."

My body froze at such news, especially her concluding request: *I'd like you to take care of Mark.* I was a deer in the headlights as my mind raced, trying to formulate a response, aware that my hackles were rising even as my heart melted a little too. Without thinking, I blurted out, "Are you asking me or telling me?"

To my amazement, Mom retained her saccharine-sweet, almost cajoling air in the face of this uncharacteristic resistance. "You know his routine, and he's so comfortable with you, he loves you, there's no one who could take care of him as well."

"What about dinner? Will I have to do the cooking too?"

"I'll put meals in the freezer, and Dad can pick up some things. Also, Aunt Claire will take you guys to the pool a couple times."

I was caught between the teenager who resented such a demand on my summer break and the inner adult who was so used to feeling capable and in control that she thrived on it. Both aspects of myself adored Mark. At three and a half, he was a peaceful child with a sense of humor and keen imagination that made him delightful company. The potential burdens and pleasures seesawed in my mind even as I perceived this was not a choice. I did not ask what the alternative plan would be if I refused her request, nor did she offer one. She might have had other approaches in mind, but my stepping up as caregiver was clearly the easiest, most efficient plan for the household. That alone leveled the seesaw for the moment, and I accepted what seemed like destiny.

"All right. I'll do it."

"Thank you," she said warmly, her smile still sweet but also now approving. I managed one in return, telling myself that this made sense and the time with Mark would be fun.

Standing in the front hall on the fourth day of the hospitalization, I caught Mark's singsong voice crooning from his room at the top of the stairs, a telltale sign that nap time was over. I pushed open the door expecting to see him sitting up in his twin bed enacting a scene with his "friends," the stuffed animals. Instead, suddenly enveloped by fragrance, I stopped short, stunned at the sight of Mark kneeling on the floor surrounded by white stuff.

"Mark!" I shrieked.

His wide brown eyes looked up at me, suddenly guilty as he returned to reality from whatever imaginary world he'd been in. My jaw dropped as I comprehended the extent and source of the mess. He had opened a tube of A+D ointment and dotted it around the entire room, including his bed, the carpet, the toy chest, and the play table. Then he had sprinkled baby powder all over these same surfaces.

"What have you done?" I roared. "Why did you do this? Didn't you go to sleep? *How could you do this?*" Pointing to the door, I barked, "Go downstairs, right now!"

"Sorry, Peg," Mark said, tears filling his eyes.

"Goddammit!" I ranted as I pulled the sheets and comforter from the bed, taking care in my rage to keep the gunk inside the fabric. Leaving the pile outside the door, I stomped down the hall to retrieve the vacuum sweeper. My hands braced on either side of my head, my own tears fell as I stared at the scene again from the doorway, adrenaline receding, and my voice grew plaintive.

"Oh my god, what a mess! How could he do this?! He never does stuff like this."

I had spent the ninety-minute nap time in the basement reading and chilling out, never in my wildest dreams anticipating that he might not sleep. Now sobs came and I dropped to my knees, shoulders shaking. This was too hard. I was only fifteen years old. How could anyone expect me to be almost solely responsible for this child for a whole week? I couldn't drive, so we were housebound unless someone came and picked us up. The day before, Mom's sister Claire had taken us to the swim club, but I didn't know how to turn off the responsibility faucet and be a kid, even though she had gladly tended Mark at the baby pool.

Sniffing, I rubbed my cheeks and perceived from this lower vantage point that the baby powder minimized the ointment's impact, so I grabbed the wastebasket and began picking up the little clumps like sausage off a pizza. Then I was able to vacuum up the remaining baby powder without difficulty. It almost began to seem funny, but not quite. With the room now restored to normal, I sat on the floor, leaned against his dresser with knees up and head bowed, eyes closed, just breathing.

Time to check on Mark, I realized with new alarm, wondering what he might have gotten into now. I gathered up the bedding and headed downstairs. Just outside the back door, I shook out the baby powder, creating misty puffs that blew toward the neighbor's house behind us. In the basement, Mark was playing with his Fisher-Price farm set, plopped on the floor, kneeling flat with his legs like a *W*, the same pose in which I had discovered him in the bedroom. He regarded me silently in sad reproach, his mouth turned down and his eyes dull. Sighing, I went around the corner, started the sheets in the washer, and returned to the family room.

"You know you should never, ever have done that, right?" I said, towering over him.

Mark nodded.

"I'm sorry I lost it. I was really upset. That mess made a lot of extra work for me."

He nodded again, his usual glint beginning to resurface. "Look, Peg," he said, "Farmer Brown is milking the cows."

"Is he? That's good. It's chore time on the farm," I said, and I sat down, encircling him with my arm and inhaling the baby-shampoo scent of his hair.

Calm was restored in that moment and for the remainder of the week, but a grudge at being asked to assume this role at all wedged itself in my gut like a rock, where it festered for months, feeding on my continued roster of responsibilities. One late fall afternoon following my piano lesson, my feet carried me toward Aunt Claire's house. She was the next oldest sister from Mom, had been widowed quite young, and raised her two daughters in a house just behind the parish school we attended. Her easygoing, accepting manner had always drawn me to her.

On this day, she and her elder daughter, Melissa, a college student, were at home. I looked up to Melissa like an older sister. Gradually the conversation spiraled beyond school happenings, and I found myself sharing how burdened I felt and broke down sobbing. Perhaps their soft eyes and listening ears breached my defenses. It was almost like being back at Grandma's. I had stopped by, unconsciously seeking a refuge, intuiting correctly that Aunt Claire could handle difficult comments about her younger sister. Like Grandma, she neither judged Ag nor denied my feelings. She patted my hand and made cooing noises of sympathy.

Melissa was direct. "I think you need to tell Aunt Ag how you feel," she said. Since it was near dinnertime, she drove me home and accompanied me to the door. I was puffy-eyed and sniffling from crying. Mom stood at the sink prepping salad for dinner when we opened the back door. Her face hardened like a statue when she saw the two of us, and my insides quivered.

"Listen to her, Aunt Ag," Melissa said, squeezing my shoulder before returning to her car.

I trembled as Mom turned steely eyes on me, and my words sounded a little breathless from nerves. "I got to talking with Melissa and Aunt Claire, and . . . I don't know . . . I just realized how overwhelmed I feel sometimes . . . it's so much sometimes, with Mark . . . everything. . . ."

She dried her hands on a towel and leaned back on the counter before responding. "Things aren't easy for me either," she said. "It's very hard on me that Dad is working so many evenings now. We have a lot less time together, and I have to do more around here."

My whole body froze as the moment became slow-motion surreal. As if removed from the entire scene, hovering above it, I saw her mouth continuing to speak but did not comprehend her words. My throat slammed closed, like a vault, but inside I screamed, *Oh my god, that's it?! All you can do is talk about yourself?*

Did minutes or only seconds pass until I reinhabited my body, once more standing just inside the kitchen door to catch her saying, ". . . so dinner will be ready in fifteen minutes." Then she moved to adjust the burner temperature under the skillet at the stove.

"Oh . . . okay," I replied tonelessly, picking up my school bag and trudging up the back steps, now with a complete understanding of my role as Ag's Daughter.

Chapter Eight

Through the rest of high school, I carried on as Ag's Daughter, grateful for the benefits and silent about the burdens. My life wasn't perfect, but I saw no choice but to accept this role as a reasonably happy ending to my mother-loss story. Though I continued to address her as Mom, in my mind I called her Ag. On a school trip to Quebec during junior year, I became good friends with a girl nicknamed Bitsy, with whom I'd played softball and volleyball in junior high. Our bond connected me to a larger group of girls in our class who socialized often at parties, while many of them valued their studies too. In their company, the feeling of being different that had dogged me since early grade school receded quite a bit. Because I was responsible and hardworking in ways that my parents approved, including working in Dad's business on weekends, they granted me a degree of freedom during high school that I did not abuse.

Ag's background in college admissions added a useful perspective to my planning when that time came. She took me on several campus tours locally and offered her expertise on courses of study. My mom resided firmly in the distant past, her death a timeline event more than half my life ago now, her memory never evoked. After graduation, I went to Dad's alma mater (now coed) and majored in English. Along the way, I studied abroad in France and discovered an interest in writing, joining the college newspaper staff my junior year and serving as editor in chief during senior year. Then I pursued a master's in journalism and landed a position in the Cincinnati office of an international human resources consulting firm. As part of the communication practice, I wrote materials presenting benefit and compensation information in everyday language.

Bitsy and I had remained close, though we had attended different colleges, and we wanted to share an apartment after I finished graduate school. She decided to buy a house, so I paid rent to live there too. The two-story light-orange brick structure had a front-porch swing that drew me right away. Even with its angular look, the house emanated a softness that said "home." There was a detached two-car garage, so we could each have a space. Located in an older middle-class municipality surrounded by the city of Cincinnati, it was close to our respective jobs downtown and our social hangouts. With three bedrooms upstairs, we each had our own, plus room for a guest. An additional little room housed the ironing board, which both of us used regularly for work clothes. The downstairs was circular, with the living room on the right, connected to the dining room behind and then to the kitchen on the back left and straight ahead from the entry.

On the June evening after we moved in, we hosted an impromptu cookout. Bitsy was one of eight children, and her family home was perpetually open for hospitality. Her mom thrived on feeding crowds. This atmosphere easily carried over to the house she and I shared, which quickly became referred to simply as "Slane" after the street where it was located. We threw many parties, but I especially loved our loosely structured daily life of shared meals and chores.

The Art of Reassembly

Very much her mother's daughter, Bitsy gravitated to food preparation and cooking in the dated kitchen at Slane, which I loved. To me, the dark laminate cabinets, frilly curtains, flowered wallpaper, and carpeted floor presented an utter lack of pretension that created ease and welcome, symbolized by the round pedestal table with four chairs that anchored the room. Many heartfelt conversations over coffee or beer occurred in the corner where it fit perfectly between two windows. For perhaps the first time in my life or at least in a long, long time, my inner and outer lives aligned. I was nearly twenty-five years old, working as a full-time professional, earning a salary, and supporting myself. Finally, my life circumstances had caught up with my maturity level, and I reveled in it, liberated.

One workday morning, I entered the kitchen to be greeted by the sight of two brown lunch bags on the counter. When I asked about it, Bitsy said, "I had all the sandwich stuff out, so it seemed silly not to go ahead and make two."

"Wow, thank you!" I said, grateful not only for a few extra minutes to eat breakfast but also the wondrous novelty of this kind gesture.

"Really, it's no big deal," she said.

"Actually, to me it is," I said quietly. "I had to make my own lunch all through school, starting in third grade."

By comparison, I already knew that each school morning, Bitsy's mom had taken individual sandwich orders from her children, part of their family lore fondly retold from time to time. Without further comment, Bitsy started making my lunch every day. The sandwiches rotated between lunch meats, most often turkey, with just the right amount of mustard or mayonnaise, sometimes with cheese, always with a sprinkling of pepper and cut into triangles. The accompaniment varied from grapes to sliced apples to cut-up melon, also veggies like carrots or red peppers. Though I expressed only routine thanks to Bitsy each morning for this kindness, inside I marveled at a seeming miracle.

Not quite a year after moving to Slane, early on a Friday morning I followed Bitsy to drop off her car for repair and then drove us both downtown. I had to stop at my office before flying out of town that afternoon, while she had a full day ahead. Heading west on Fourth Street, I pulled over on the right side to let her out opposite the bank where she worked. She wished me a great trip and went around the back of the car to cross the street. I pulled ahead a half block, intending to turn right at the intersection, but just before I reached it, there was a terrible, terrible *thump* of impact.

"*No . . . please, no!*" I said aloud to myself, panic rising inside. But I knew. Without thinking I pulled over and jumped out, and there she was, lying in the middle of the street, her purse and tote bag beside her. I saw her attempt to get up, a dazed, almost vacant look on her face. But she was unable to muster all the necessary motions to stand. Bystanders were already gathering. A woman crouched next to her speaking soothingly.

Fear held my entire body in a vise, but I forced my legs to walk toward the scene. As sirens became audible in the distance, rational thought kicked in: *I should notify her parents.* I ran into the bank and used the phone in the lobby. Bitsy's mom answered with her characteristic cheerfulness, and my heart squeezed.

Breathless, I managed to state, "Bitsy was hit by a car crossing Fourth Street after I dropped her off. She is definitely injured, but I don't think it's life-threatening. An ambulance is coming." Ruth remained composed, for which I was thankful. She asked only one or two questions and named a particular hospital. Hanging up, the reality that I had a plane to catch in a few hours occurred to me, followed by another rational thought: *Someone else will have to accompany Bitsy in the ambulance.* I took the elevator to the fourth floor, explained to her coworkers what was happening, and asked her friend Nancy to ride to the hospital.

The two of us returned to the street just in time to see Bitsy being placed on a stretcher. The sight of her in a cervical neck collar made my knees feel weak. *I really have no idea how seriously she's injured*, I thought. After conveying the hospital information, I waited until the ambulance departed before returning to my car—which I had left unlocked with keys in the ignition and my purse on the front seat—and drove the few more blocks to my own office, where there were client projects to wrap up in preparation for a week of vacation.

My colleagues all knew Bitsy and were quick to offer support. "Peg, my brother-in-law is an EMT. They use cervical collars as a precaution all the time. Don't assume that means anything bad." The anxiety of not knowing the extent of her injuries numbed my limbs and constricted my chest, and I could not concentrate on the tasks I needed to accomplish. Neither could I overcome the fear of learning the truth about Bitsy's condition. Seeing my distress, without telling me, my friend Linda called the emergency room, spoke to a family member, and brought me concrete facts: broken leg, broken nose, bruises and contusions, damaged teeth. Bitsy was banged up, but she would heal. My exhale of relief ushered in trembling and a few tears, clearing my mind enough to focus on phone calls and memos. Then I went home to finish packing before Dad and Mark came to pick me up. Mark and I were traveling to visit Tim on Nantucket, where he was working. As I stepped into the kitchen from the back door, the sheer ordinariness of our mugs on the counter, still half-full of milky coffee now gone cold, pierced my heart, but I did not allow myself to cry. There wasn't time. I had a plane to catch.

We experienced travel delays and chilly, rainy weather on our vacation, so Mark and I had to work hard at entertaining ourselves. Several times during the trip, I called Bitsy's family to receive updates. Early in the week, she had surgery to insert a rod in her leg to stabilize the bone for healing and was in a lot of pain after. She left the hospital the day I came home and went to stay at her parents for a few days. Determined to resume a normal life, she soon returned to the house we shared and went back to work. With her right leg uninjured and her left leg casted only up to the knee, Bitsy was able to drive and began exercising on a stationary bike at a YMCA since she couldn't go out running. She quickly became adept on crutches and insisted on doing as many tasks as possible, especially in the kitchen. The lunch bags appeared on the counter again within a short interval.

I did not bounce back so readily. With great effort, I had kept myself together on the trip, but back at home I cried easily and often. Tears stung my eyes while waving goodbye to Bitsy when she left for work or to visit a friend or while alone in my own office gazing at the city from the eighteenth floor. Opening my packed lunch in the break room and then putting it back in the refrigerator after only a few bites, pulling into the driveway at Principio to have dinner with my family—anything could spark weeping. Perhaps, I rationalized, it was just letdown brought on by the stressful vacation undertaken amid emotional upset. However, over time I noticed the disproportion of my reaction relative to Bitsy's situation and to how others were handling it. Inside, I felt lost and empty, as if I were falling, falling, falling through space. These sensations were strangely familiar in a way I could not quite identify.

One hot, shimmery morning in mid-July, I came downstairs to the kitchen dressed for work in a short-sleeved cotton flowered dress with a flared skirt. Bitsy was already at the table eating breakfast.

She looked up from her cereal bowl and said, "You cannot wear that dress."

"What do you mean? Why?" I asked, glancing down in search of a fallen hem or stain.

"Have you looked in the mirror? It's too big. It's hanging on you like a sack. You've lost too much weight."

Maybe she was right, but I really didn't feel like changing. "It will be fine for today."

"At least go upstairs and get that green scarf out of my top drawer and put it around your waist like a belt, so it won't look so shapeless," Bitsy said, which I did and noticed the improvement.

All my clothes were loose, though I was not trying to lose weight. Something was happening. For the first time, a quiet curiosity about myself began to stir. A nascent inner voice wondered, *What's this about?* Finally, understanding dawned.

The lost and falling feeling was the way I had felt right after my mom died, an astonishing realization. It had been nearly twenty years since her death. Could I really be reacting to something that happened so long ago? Was this what grief felt like?

I shared this discovery with Bitsy over dinner at the kitchen table.

"It makes sense, Peg," she said immediately.

"It's as if the accident toppled my insides. Like an earthquake. I can't just put it back the way it was."

By August, the most acute weepiness had abated, but a constant vague disquiet hovered. I needed help. This grief or whatever it was would not just go away by itself like a cold, and I began seeing a therapist recommended by a coworker. Over many sessions, I told Dr. Jackson about my mom's illness, how I didn't know she was dying, the terrible morning I learned that she was gone, and how the free-falling sensation returned after my friend's accident had knocked it all loose.

Legs crossed, her chin resting on her closed hand, Dr. Jackson regarded me through horn-rimmed glasses, the picture of poise as my words spilled out. Occasionally she nodded or asked for clarification, but a certain knitting of her brows accompanied by pursed lips signaled a more probing question. Then I would stiffen slightly, bracing myself.

"So how would you describe your childhood then?"

"It definitely had sad parts, but I feel lucky that I had people who took care of me, like my grandma and my dad, and then after Dad remarried, I had a mom again."

She cocked her head as if to say, *Really?*

"What do you want me to say? I'm telling you my experience!"

She looked at me, considering, then finally said, "I think you have a tendency to 'coach' your emotions to fit a desired scenario."

Shrugging, I turned to the window as my insides bristled, but I stuck to my story. I was not ready to challenge the happy ending.

PART TWO

Chapter Nine

A college friend visiting from out of town, shortly before the accident, had insisted that Bitsy's older brother Joe was attracted to me.

"It's in his eyes, Peg."

To which I replied, "I could never marry Joe Conway. He doesn't like to go to parties and have fun the way I do. It would never work." Secretly though, I found myself quite enamored of his kindness and whimsical sense of humor.

During Bitsy's recuperation, close friends came for dinner often, especially Joe. We would grill out in the backyard and lounge around the picnic table. They were the sort of evenings where you laughed the whole time and then later could not remember why.

He never expressed concerns aloud, but following the accident, I sensed Joe's intentional care for both Bitsy and me. It *was* in his brown eyes, crinkly with laughter beneath dark eyebrows and curly hair, and in his acts of service like refilling my drink without being asked, manning the grill, clearing the table, and loading the dishwasher afterward. Gradually, over that summer, Joe and I began speaking on the phone regularly, then progressed to making separate plans to attend group events or go on bike rides or to concerts on our own.

Trust came easily. I had already known him for several years because he'd lived with his parents while completing his PhD. Without hesitation, I shared the emotional turmoil that Bitsy's accident had triggered. He listened attentively but didn't dwell on the hardship alone. Rather, his awareness reached beyond loss and grief to include my mom as a person. Without any prompting, he referred to her by her name, Mary Lee. No one else ever did, I was startled to realize. This simple gesture moved me deeply.

His support emboldened me. On an overcast autumn Sunday, I asked Joe to go with me to the cemetery to see my mom's grave, which I had never visited. On the drive out, I realized that we had no idea of her grave location in the sprawling suburban cemetery, and the office would be closed. My enthusiasm began to wane, but Joe was certain we could find her by looking for other graves from around the year of her death. Once we parked the car and started walking around, we soon realized the flaw in our methodology. Anyone experienced in visiting cemeteries knows that people are not buried according to chronology. Families, or at least couples, tend to be together, so generations spanning several decades might lie next to one another.

As we wandered around in the crisp air, the sight of many familiar names evoked a stream of memories, and it reminded me of the final scene in Thornton Wilder's play, *Our Town*, where the main character has died, and at the cemetery, she wanders through the action, unseen by the others, but exclaiming aloud as she recognizes people from her past. We became so absorbed in these discoveries that we almost forgot our real purpose for coming. Rounding the last corner of the section we had been searching and heading back to the car, we grew philosophical.

"We'll have to come back sometime when the office is open or call to get the location."

Then suddenly her name was in my face, as if the letters on the marker had leapt in the air. "There she is," I whispered, pointing just ahead.

Not ten feet behind where we had parked, in the opposite direction from which we had started walking, was my mom's grave. We were transfixed for a moment, almost paralyzed. Then I could hardly breathe, feeling joy, fear, and peace all at once. My mother's gravestone sat on a very slight, almost imperceptible rise in the ground, just enough to distinguish her marker from all those around her. It felt as if she were reaching out to me, and I was astonished. Laughing and crying at the same time, Joe and I just stood there, hugging. This powerful shared experience created a private space where my mom could exist as a present-day memory. She was real to Joe, and he accepted my mother loss, including its emotional fallout, as simply facts of life.

About fourteen months after Bitsy's accident, Joe presented me with a diamond ring, and I said, "Yes!" Throughout our engagement, Ag's training through the years came in most useful. When my cousin Melissa had married when I was in high school, I had been thrilled to be in the wedding party and witness it all first-hand—the showers, gift registry, gift opening, thank-you notes, rehearsal and rehearsal dinner, toasts, flowers, dresses, dancing. Now it was my turn. Soon after Joe and I were engaged, we met my parents for a drink after work to discuss wedding plans. This outer process seemed normal and expected, unrelated to my inner mother grief, which I guarded carefully.

On the wedding logistics, I knew Ag would come prepared, and she did not disappoint. Before delving into her research, she opened with a general question. "Do you have a preference on day or evening for the wedding?"

Joe and I had discussed this, so I replied for both of us, "We were thinking afternoon, since Joe is not much of a party guy. He prefers that, which is fine with me."

Ag looked over at my dad, who nodded, and she picked up her notes before continuing. My eyes glazed over as she went on about the estimated number of guests, the pros and cons of various venues, and caterer options. Joe listened politely, equally dulled by the details, I could tell.

Pausing to shuffle her notes and regard us both directly, Ag said, "So, if you're comfortable with this general approach, are you okay if I handle the details for the reception? We can visit the venues together and make that decision as a group, but after that . . . ?"

Joe's relieved expression matched my own, so I answered immediately, "That sounds great. We'd like to focus on planning the ceremony."

In the car with Joe afterward, I commented, "I hope you're okay with this division of responsibilities. You seemed like you agreed. I'm fine with her having control over that part of the event, if that's what she wants, and you know she'll see to the minutiae. I don't have time for all that anyway."

"I have total confidence in Ag to organize the reception!" Joe said, laughing.

A few weeks later, my stomach twisted in an unfamiliar knot as Bitsy drove us to the bridal shop on a Saturday morning. Ag had orchestrated this outing after pressing me on the need to get my wedding dress ordered.

"You have to allow up to twelve weeks," she had emphasized, "plus time for alterations."

Like our past shopping excursions, Ag had conducted an exploratory mission resulting in a set of preselected dresses for me to try on, so now here we were. After a quick greeting, the saleswoman swept us to the back dressing room area. Bitsy and

Ag chatted while the saleswoman assisted me into the first dress. Stepping out of the cubicle to model before the mirrors, the syrupy pride in Ag's face prompted a silent prayer of thanks for Bitsy's presence here to soften this "mother-daughter" moment. Our prior shopping outings, which had continued into my graduate school years, had felt nurturing. Now, in the ongoing emotional wake of Bitsy's accident, confusion had emerged. Was Ag my mother, or were we playacting?

Both Ag and Bitsy regarded the dress and then searched my face, querying without words.

"It's nice," I said, "but it doesn't really grab me."

One after the other, we all mostly agreed the dresses either did not suit or merely elicited no enthusiasm. However, Ag and I locked wills over the wearing of veils and trains with the dress.

"Oh, but they're traditional," she said, focusing in on the train. "How can you think of not wearing one?"

"I really don't want all that. I've been a bridesmaid and seen what a bother it is for the bride. Trains are silly." Given the practicality of her own bridal wear, I found her insistence on a train rather mystifying and said so.

"That was different," she said. "We were older."

Out of Ag's view, I rolled my eyes at Bitsy, who suppressed a laugh. The saleswoman, who had been listening without comment, left to peruse the racks for more options. Returning with a bright white satin dress, she said, "This is a size fourteen and on closeout, so we can't order it anymore. It will be quite big, but it can be altered."

She helped me into the dress and fastened large clips at the back to approximate the correct fit. Though I had been unable to specify my desires, this dress was perfect. Long sleeved with a sweetheart-style neckline, it had large puffs at the shoulders that balanced its otherwise straight look. I liked how it was fitted at the waist with a straight but not fitted skirt. Generous beads and sequins added elegance, but fundamentally it was a dress in which I could move about easily.

The saleswoman said, "I'm almost afraid to say this, but it does come with a train that attaches with Velcro, so you could wear it during the ceremony at church and then remove it for ease at the reception."

Ag's eyes started to light up, but I shook my head, grinning. "So, I could whip it off at the end and toss it at the congregation if I wanted? Nope. I'm not wearing the train, and Bitsy's friend from her tennis team will make me a simple headpiece."

Ag compressed her lips but said nothing more about trains or veils. After I had dressed again in my street clothes, we waited at the front desk to pay and schedule the alterations. Suddenly a long-ago special dress came to mind, an artifact from the past. The spring after my mom died, her youngest sister, Jeanne, purchased my first communion dress, shopping on her lunch hour downtown. I had informed her that I didn't want a baby-looking dress that tied in the back and had short puffy sleeves. She found me a straight dress, with scalloped embroidery, chiffon sleeves, and a soft bow at the neck that I loved so much. My wedding dress evoked the same feeling. Perfect for me. I smiled inside, warmed by the gift of recollection.

Chapter Ten

As newlyweds, Joe and I moved into a two-bedroom apartment in a blue-frame row house, one of six in varied colors lined up together on a busy incline just north of downtown, close to my office and not far from the university where Joe was teaching in the business school on a one-year contract. Our apartment ran along the back of the building on the second floor, entered at the top of a long flight of carpeted stairs. There was a small living room and an eat-in kitchen with two windows, one of which overlooked the parking lot where neighborhood guys regularly gathered for "car nights," with front hoods up and tools scattered about. A hallway led to the bathroom on the right and then the bedrooms at the end on either side. Though the cream walls and tan carpet throughout were bland, we delighted in creating our first home together.

We both felt ready to have a baby. Joe was thirty-one, and I was twenty-seven, and we saw no reason to wait. Becoming pregnant about three months after our wedding elicited euphoria and terror all at once for me. The exponential risk of loss associated with bringing a precious new being into the world took my breath away even as my heart thrilled with excitement. At this juncture, my life was a clean canvas, an expansive white space on which I would write my own story. It was my turn to narrate, and I would do everything in my power to ensure our children felt safe and loved. I would do things right. Choosing to birth with midwives fit with this goal. Though this approach to maternity care departed from many of my friends' choices, for once I valued difference. I would accept nothing unthinkingly when it came to our baby.

Starting at the fourth week of pregnancy, nausea permeated my days. First thing in the morning, I had to eat crackers with a dab of peanut butter while still lying in bed, then sit up to sip ginger ale before I could arise. Just getting ready for work and out the door each morning required the effort of scaling a cliff. Throughout the day I needed strategically timed snacks to abate the sick feelings. I did not throw up but constantly felt on the brink of it. I was also exhausted all the time and thankful for an office with a door that I could close when I needed to put my head on the desk for a power nap.

Joe placed the crackers and ginger ale on the night stand each morning, made breakfast, packed my lunch (I could stomach only plain turkey on wheat with light mayo), and drove me the mile and a half to and from the office, all of which gave me the time I needed just to get my physical body minimally functioning for the workday. He mothered me in other ways too. The second oldest in their family of eight children, he had often assisted his mother in the kitchen. He enjoyed cooking and had a flexible work schedule, so he did all the grocery shopping and cooked dinner too.

Sometimes I received his care graciously, like an adult, but often I reacted as a petulant child when the menu did not match my unpredictable food cravings and aversions. I sobbed in frustration when my expanding girth outgrew yet another skirt and melted down in a tantrum when the guy living above us turned on thumping music first thing in the morning or at night when I was trying to sleep. Joe remained kind and forbearing; he patiently listened and comforted. Again, sometimes I could appreciate these gestures as a grown-up, but regularly they only fanned my childish flames. Couldn't he get mad on my behalf at our inconsiderate neighbor? Didn't he care? Eventually I would cry it out, and shaky calm would descend, but this recurring cycle of tension and release left me bewildered. Who was I? Where did my self-control go? Why couldn't I cope? I never knew what would trigger the Inner Lost Girl.

"Will I ever get over this?" I asked Dr. Jackson.

She allowed a beat of quiet before replying gently, "In time, the intensity will lessen, but yes, I think issues of loss will always be significant for you."

Throughout the pregnancy, after a midwife appointment, having connected with their quiet calm and heard the *swish-swish* of our baby's heartbeat, I trusted my body. At home on my own, I fretted over whatever birth defect or nutritional deficiency I had just read about in *What to Expect When You're Expecting*. Joe received a running commentary reflecting these two mental poles. Trained in chemistry and business, he was a thinker, and his personality allowed him to dwell more easily in the present moment than I could. Plus, he hadn't experienced traumatic loss in early life. Often, I would ask him to quell my worries.

"Please be rational for me here. Tell me why I don't need to obsess over this," I'd say, and he would offer a reasonable-sounding reassurance. Late in the second trimester he finally suggested, teasing but with a little exasperation, "I think you should put away the books. Just stop reading about all this stuff." I saw his point and tried to heed the advice.

Labor began early on a Friday, just two days before my due

date. Our son Michael was born in the early morning of February 22, 1992, after a long night of excruciating low-back pain due to his head position, followed by a lengthy pushing stage. Even though I was totally spent, the instant my hands felt his sturdy back and I gazed into his dark eyes, I fell in love. In a wondering voice, I repeated over and over, "Isn't he beautiful?"

We went home early the following afternoon. Joe pulled up on the street in front of our apartment, and I walked gingerly up the stairs, one at a time with pauses in between, gripping the bannister. Joe carried Michael in his car seat and unloaded all the gear, which somehow had multiplied tenfold since our departure from home just thirty-six hours before. The jubilation of giving birth soon gave way to the reality of postpartum recovery and life with a newborn.

Joe's mom provided a casserole that his sister brought over that afternoon. I sat down to eat and managed two bites before Michael started fussing and crying. Right that instant I realized: *This is my life now.* Already I wished that babies came with an off button so I could have fifteen minutes to eat a meal. By eleven at night, my breasts had become hard, hot boulders when my milk came in like a tsunami. Michael could not latch on, and he was crying, nearly inconsolable. I hurt everywhere, and just then the post-birth adrenaline drop conveniently occurred. Exhausted, I broke down in despair of ever being able to breastfeed and at a complete loss of what to do.

At midnight we phoned the midwives and thanked our lucky stars that Karen, our favorite, was on call for the whole weekend.

"He's hungry," she said. "Give him a little formula. You should have samples from discharge. It will be all right. Put hot compresses on your breasts to soften them. Then, when he's ready to eat again, dribble a little formula on your nipple as he's latching on."

Now we had a plan. It worked partially, but I could not get my milk flowing easily, even though there was plenty there. The next couple days were a blur of phone calls and consultations with midwives, nurses, and friends until supply and demand finally evened out. On Monday, Joe had to rally through fatigue to teach classes. He said a cheerful goodbye that belied his haggard appearance, leaning to kiss my cheek as I sat on the couch with Michael. "Bye, sweetie, have a good day," he said. "I love you."

"Love you too. See you later," I said, fighting tears and reaching up for a quick hug.

I heard his steps fading down the stairs and then the slam of the building's front door, leaving me alone for the first time with our newborn. Everything I needed was close at hand: cup of water to my right, receiving blankets and burp cloths stacked to my left, and the baby seat nearby on the floor. Michael was sleeping soundly for the moment, his head in the crook of my left arm, which rested on a pillow. *Just take it one thing at a time*, I bolstered myself, trying to quell habitual anxiety about sudden loss. What if Joe died in a car accident? What if I dropped Michael? An hour later, as planned, Ag arrived just as Michael roused. His arms flailed near his head like usual, but something seemed off in his movements.

"His face looks really red to me. Do you think he looks all right?" I asked, as my whole body tingled. "Is he struggling to breathe?" I stared at my baby, trying to discern if this was imagined distress or mother's intuition. "He's had a lot of mucous."

Ag studied him, her face impassive. No cues there. "I think he seems okay," she said. Regardless, escalating panic took over.

"I'm going to call 911."

She nodded solemnly. "If that's what you think."

After I hung up with the dispatcher, Ag said, "You might keep him upright to promote drainage."

The Art of Reassembly

I repositioned Michael on my shoulder. Moments later four burly EMTs tromped up the steps into our little apartment, their presence filling the small, square living room. By then Michael's skin tone and affect had returned to normal. We all stood as I held Michael and explained what happened. Then the leader assessed Michael briefly with a stethoscope. Peering into Michael's face, he shrugged lightly and looked back at me with kind eyes.

"Ma'am, do you want transport to the hospital for him to be checked out? I don't see cause for concern at this point, but it's up to you."

I felt so silly. "No, I think he's fine too. I'm sorry to have dragged you out over nothing."

"Never hesitate to call. That is what we're here for," he said, smiling and patting Michael on the head. "You take care."

"Well, that was exciting," I said to Ag wryly after they had gone, covering my embarrassment with humor.

"I'm glad he's fine. You needed to be sure."

Michael had started fussing, so I returned to the couch to feed him, which added to my unease. Though Ag and I had tended a baby together years before, breastfeeding was not part of that shared experience, leaving her without expertise in this area. That she averted her face ever so slightly as I attempted to latch Michael on communicated her discomfort with it. A yawning silence prevailed as I concentrated on my task, and Ag sat in the club chair. I could have retreated to the bedroom, but leaving her alone seemed more uncomfortable than staying there. We passed the afternoon politely. I appreciated her presence so I could take a shower and rest, but a new awkwardness had entered the scene.

When I was a kid, home alone or with no adults nearby, our tall dark-green metal file cabinet drew me like a magnet. It held our family photos from the period before Dad's remarriage. Hefty and quite old, its drawers closed with a slow but resounding *thump* that I loved. At our house on Raeburn, where the filing cabinet was in the utility room, and then later in the basement at Principio, I would pull open the second-from-the-bottom drawer, breathe in its comforting musty smell, and carefully peruse the bright yellow Kodak envelopes that contained photos documenting the growth of our family from the late 1950s to the early 1970s. I've always relished museums and archives, but in these clandestine forays I ached over and over for something that I could not name.

Over the early weeks of motherhood, beyond mastering breastfeeding and diapering, it was attuning to Michael's personality that boosted my confidence the most. As I fed him in the dark of three in the morning, I marveled at how far we had come already. Before becoming a mother, I could never have imagined fulfilling such round-the-clock needs for anyone, even with the level of support Joe provided. Then, *bam!* Insight hit me like a brick: *Somewhere inside, I knew how to do this. I must have received it sometime, somewhere. Oh, yes . . . of course. My mom loved me exactly the way I love my precious baby.* I gulped in breaths, overcome by this unsought answer to my unstated longing. If I had been standing, I would have doubled over. Instead, I snuggled Michael more closely and kissed the top of his head, as my feet rocked us lightly back and forth in the chair.

Chapter Eleven

"Hey, Mark! How's it going?" I said, coming up from the basement of my family's home with two-month-old Michael on my shoulder. Laundry facilities for our row-house apartment were located several buildings away. Rather than try to surmount this obstacle with a tiny baby in tow, I would pack up Michael and the dirty clothes and head here or to Bitsy's to accomplish the chore under less-taxing circumstances. We had been alone here this afternoon before Mark's arrival. Ag was at work.

Mark sat at the breakfast room table, silent, fiddling with a piece of junk mail. He did not look up as we entered, and I closed the basement door behind me. A sophomore at the Catholic boys' school that three generations of our relatives had attended, Mark was no longer the little boy I had doted on. Already more than six feet tall, his frequently stooped posture witnessed to his self-consciousness about it. Mark was growing his hair long, and shapeless bangs obscured his eyes and any facial expression.

When he did not respond to my pleasantries, I accepted teen moodiness. At a second glance, though, his whole body seemed coiled. Tension in his long fingers increased as he stopped crumpling the direct-mail postcard and instead began tearing it into small pieces. Then I heard him sniff and realized he was crying.

"Mark, what's wrong?!"

He spoke tersely from behind the curtain of hair, as though even saying the words hurt, like plunging a knife in his own side, "I was cut from the tennis team. The very last person. Again. Just like last year."

"Oh no! I'm so sorry!"

I set Michael in his car seat and wrapped my arms around Mark, but it was like hugging a telephone pole. His crying did not escalate, though tears continued to quietly stream down his cheeks. He said nothing else and did not lean into me for comfort. This unfamiliar, withdrawn Mark unnerved me. I felt powerless to console him at all, and tears leaked from my eyes. I held him a minute longer and kissed the top of his head.

Then simmering anger blazed from beneath his frozen veneer. He threw down the scraps of postcard, pounded his fist on the table, and bellowed, "*I hate that coach so fucking much!*"

Michael started crying at the outburst as Mark pushed back his chair and stomped into the living room and up the stairs to his room, slamming the door. Trembling, I picked Michael up, clutched him against my chest, and rocked from side to side, trying to calm both of us. He nuzzled my neck, signaling his desire to nurse, so I went to the living room alcove and sat in the easy chair where I had given baby Mark so many bottles, my cheeks damp and my whole being flooded with distress. Mark would not come out of his room or speak to me further. Before departing with our clean clothes piled in a basket, I stood outside his door and said, "I love you, sweetie."

That evening, I talked to Ag on the phone, reporting in detail on my interaction with Mark. She asked speculative questions that

I could not possibly answer. "Did he find out during the school day or right after? What do you think the coach said to him? Do you think he yelled at the coach?" Frustrated and not seeing the point of these queries, I tried to be patient because of the frantic undertone I sensed beneath her words. Over the ensuing weeks, Joe and I would learn that Mark was failing two classes in school, which was unprecedented. He had always been a good student. Worried, I was determined to keep tabs on the situation.

The addition of Michael soon overcrowded our compact apartment, so during my maternity leave, Joe and I began looking at houses. We quickly homed in on a listing down the street from his cousin Marjorie and her husband and four children. Overlooking the dated decor, we chose to appreciate its several bedrooms and fenced backyard, the tree-lined sidewalks, and the walkable distance to the public library. Because we had no deadline for moving, we acceded to the sellers' request to close a few months later, allowing for the completion of their new home. We would move in the late summer. I was back at work as we considered two weekends at the end of August, and for some reason I kept pressing for the earlier weekend. Joe didn't have a strong preference, so he agreed. Though it made the timeline more pressured, with help from friends and family we pulled it off. It would be weeks if not months before we were truly settled, but the beginnings of home took root.

Just three days after our move, Joe called me at the office because Ag had phoned our house, breathless and shaken, with Mark on an angry rampage, knocking over lamps and destroying a framed picture on the wall. Joe was not teaching that day, so he asked our friend to watch Michael while he went over there. Ultimately, he brought Mark to our house. Over the four months

since we had learned about Mark's failing grades, we had become
a safety valve for Mark and my parents. Joe or I often drove Mark
to therapy appointments, begun at the suggestion of his school
counselor, and the therapist had quickly diagnosed depression.

"Well, thank God we moved last weekend," I said to Joe as we
collapsed into bed after an exhausting evening of serving dinner,
setting up a bed for Mark, and dealing with his school logistics
on top of the emotional drain of trying to maintain composure.
In the privacy of our bed, I cried on Joe's shoulder to release the
strain.

"There's nothing else we can do about this right now. He
calmed down as soon as we left their house, and things are stable
for the moment. We need to go to sleep and think about it again
tomorrow," Joe said, stroking my back.

"I know, I know, you're right," I replied, sniffing back tears
and exhaling. "Thanks honey, I love you."

Mark stayed with us for a tense week, during which he vacil-
lated between relief at escaping parental conflict and bitterness at
the forced exile. Delicately, we pointed out that his own behavior
had precipitated the situation and that he had some control over
how things would proceed from here. Negotiations orchestrated
with his therapist ultimately allowed his return home. Meanwhile,
because of our move, a much longer daily commute caused me
to miss Michael terribly. I craved contact with his wiggly, pudgy
body, yearned to see him smile and hear his coos. Three months
later, just before Christmas, I quit working to become a stay-at-
home mom.

In my youth, besides the packets of Kodak envelopes, the
beloved green file cabinet housed a cream-colored album with
black paper pages. Its black-and-white photos affixed with triangular stickers documented my eldest brother's first year. Though
this book was least interesting to me as a child, my life as a young

mother with a dark-eyed, round-faced baby boy came to mirror its content as Michael became a toddler. Our days were filled with outings to the park, a weekly play group in the neighborhood, and playtime in the backyard sandbox, slide, and plastic pool. I didn't know what to think or feel about the uncanny similarity with my mom's situation.

Joe shifted careers too, not long after I quit my job. He began working in his family's restaurant company, initially as a management trainee in the actual restaurant. While I sought these role changes and embraced them, I had no idea what they would require of me as our story continued to unfold.

Chapter Twelve

Not long after quitting work, I became pregnant again, due the following October. At one of my early midwife appointments, I told Karen that I didn't feel like taking childbirth classes this time. Logistically it would be challenging with a toddler and a husband who worked a lot of nights, but I wanted to prepare somehow. Her cornflower eyes gazed at me thoughtfully for a minute before she said, "Gayle Peterson has a new book out. It's called *Easier Birth*, or something like that. You might check that out."

A few weeks later, I settled on the couch while Michael napped, *An Easier Childbirth: A Mother's Guide for Birthing Normally* open in my lap. More of a workbook than a how-to, it started out with a questionnaire that asked me to consider my present situation and plans for the birth. Yes, I trusted my caregiver and felt good about birth plans. Yes, I had a strong, supportive relationship with my partner. Yes, I felt confident in my body.

In the second section, I stopped short at the question asking me to rate "relationship with mother," both currently and in childhood. How was I to respond? Based on Mary Lee, who died when I was seven, or Ag, my adoptive/stepmom of nearly twenty years? One for childhood and the other for now? Although a zero rating seemed to best describe my real mother, its meaning unsettled me: "very painful, little or no contact, absence or abandonment as the major association." As for Ag, it was hard to characterize our relationship. Was it 1) "nurturing in some ways, but with frequent struggle"? Or 2) "positive feelings, but ambivalent about spending too much time with her"? Or possibly 3) "mostly positive feelings of warmth and understanding, with minor disagreement"?

Ag and I maintained a friendly front, but inevitably our dealings about Mark weighed down the relationship. It strained the cozy trio of our prior history, replacing it with an unhealthy triangle. Regularly she called me on the phone to fact find. After high-pitched chitchat, she would drop the false cheer to pose the dreaded, "Have you talked to Mark?" that I knew from the outset was coming.

Uncertain what to say without knowing the purpose of her query, I would stay noncommittal. "Yes, we talked the other day."

"Did he tell you about that concert he wants to go to in Indianapolis next weekend?" He had not, so I could truthfully say so, relieved.

"Well, I'd appreciate if you would tell him it's not a good idea to go. He's got that term paper due the following week, and I just really don't want him to go."

My stomach knotted, and inwardly I squirmed, hating this middle position, but I was learning to shield against further inroads.

"If an opportunity presents itself, I'll try to mention it," I said. A loud silence followed.

"Okay, thanks," she replied finally, in a controlled voice, and I knew my response displeased her.

"Oh, Michael's awake. I hear him crying upstairs. I've got to go," I said, grateful for the diversion.

Initially the triangular situation with Ag and Mark only caused discomfort, but later I would hang up the phone feeling used and resentful. Though he never actually lived with us except the one brief time, Mark carved out his own place in our household, almost as though I'd had a child prior to being married to Joe. We stocked canned New England clam chowder and hot sauce because he liked them. At least once a week he would come for dinner. Afterward, I would clean up, and Joe would bring out his whiteboard and markers. Seated side by side on the living room couch, whiteboard across their laps, Joe would take the science or math textbook from Mark and say, "Okay, what've you got?"

As the tutoring proceeded, Michael moved back and forth between kitchen and couch, first crawling and then toddling about as Mark, grinning, accepted toys and books from him, glad for momentary distraction from the calculations on the whiteboard. When Michael eventually tired and became fussy, I would scoop him up and put him to bed. Sometimes Mark went home shortly after, but often he ascended to our third floor to use the computer and departed long after we had gone to bed, using his own key to lock up. In the morning, I might find a paper to edit for him on the dining room table.

Mark still experienced intermittent dark periods that stretched my heart to the breaking point. Confronted with an inert teenager slumped on the couch, I became increasingly frustrated at monotone answers, frequently "I don't know" again and again, while my mind shrieked, *Why don't you do something? Why did you wait until the last minute to think about this?*

However, reading library books had educated me about depression's insidiousness, and I learned to regularly set aside my concerns for Mark and go outdoors with Michael to breathe fresh air and walk vigorously, pushing the stroller around the neighborhood.

Instinctively, I protected myself and withheld these depths from Ag in our strained phone conversations.

"I guess you and Joe are pretty worn out from all this."

"Well, we're all doing our best."

In time I reached a limit and could not hear anymore over-tures like "I need you to tell Mark . . . ." Or worse, "What has Mark said about . . . ?" Or "Do you know what Mark is planning to do about . . . ?"

Finally, the necessary words rose to the surface. "You're going to have to ask him yourself. He is practically a grown-up. I can't be your go-between."

"Oh, yes, I see," she replied, her icy tone conveying all that her words left unspoken.

That afternoon with my birth-preparation workbook, pon-dering my relationship with Ag and my dead mom, I realized that all the possible ratings applied to me: nurturing, abandonment, positive feelings, and disagreement. I felt such ambivalence at introducing this enormous topic into my birth-preparation pro-cess at all. Reflecting my uncertainty, I wrote question marks next to 0, 1, 2, and 3 and turned the page.

The next section proved the most challenging. "Briefly describe any anxiety you may have about loss or abandonment in childhood . . . may include parental divorce, death." My body tensed with desire to distance from this question. In truth, the Inner Lost Girl manifested often as the pregnancy progressed, from just a few tears to a full meltdown depending on my fatigue and hormone levels and the circumstances. Commonly, she cried when Joe left to work his long restaurant shifts from midafternoon to early morning. She felt abandoned when I had to do dinner prep and cleanup plus toddler bath and bedtime all by myself.

Even more painfully, I had begun to observe the significance of mothers in the lives of their adult daughters and grandchildren, how bonds of warmth and love extended across three generations, and I recollected my grandma taking care of us before and after my mom died. I just didn't have that. Soon after Michael's birth, Ag had returned to full-time work, and the tensions around Mark continued to shift our terrain. Once again, I felt different from my peers, in a way I hadn't experienced since the first few years after my mom's death. In the privacy of my living room, I recorded that my mom died when I was seven years old. Then it was time to close the book and do a few chores before Michael woke up.

Labor started early on the morning of October 14, and our daughter, Kieran, arrived in the wee hours of the next day. The process built gradually but finished swiftly, just fifteen minutes after we got to the hospital. With a dazed smile, I announced softly from my squatting position, "Oh, it's a girl." Joe beamed in relief at the contrast with Michael's protracted delivery as he cradled her in his arms, but mental images of giving birth in the car if we hadn't made it in time tempered my joy a little. Doubts began to form minutes after her birth as I gazed at Kieran's perfect pink form. Was I even capable of mothering a daughter? Coming after Mark and Michael, a baby girl felt foreign. Would I know what to do? I was grateful that Joe had arranged to take four weeks of family leave right after the birth.

Chapter Thirteen

On the Tuesday before Thanksgiving, our neighbor Marjorie watched both kids while Joe and I went out together. Looking ahead to Joe's resuming a busy work schedule, we opted to shop for the kids' Christmas gifts. Marjorie greeted us on our return with Kieran in the crook of her arm and reported that she had slept a lot and was a bit warm. Pushing back against reflexive fear, I rationalized: Maybe Kieran's starting a growth spurt, or perhaps she was wrapped in too many blankets. This was midafternoon. By evening, Kieran was unmistakably radiating heat like a baked potato. She was also lethargic and had hardly eaten. Joe took her temperature, and it was 102 degrees. I phoned our pediatrician's on-call number only to be instructed firmly: "Take her to Children's Hospital."

"What?!"

"An infant under six weeks with a fever must be taken to the emergency room."

Now I was trembling. This could not be happening. We hastily arranged for Marjorie's teenaged daughter to come down and stay with Michael. She was off school the next day for the holiday so able to sleep over if needed. Once again, we drove down a dark highway to a hospital, this time filled with a sick dread vastly different than five weeks before while I'd been in labor with Kieran. At Children's Hospital, the emergency room staff was neither alarmist nor reassuring.

A nurse explained, "Their bodies are so small, with an infection they can get very sick very quickly, so that's why you have to bring her here."

Therefore, Kieran must have a full septic workup. They wanted us to leave the room because "it's easier." *Yes, it is easier for you but not for my daughter.* At my insistence, they relented. I knew from the midwives that hearing mama's voice always consoles babies, and I clung desperately to this belief as she was pricked and poked. I held her still during these painful procedures, first in my lap while they took blood and then flat on her back, for a catheterized urine sample. Though I spoke tender words in her ear, this intended comfort felt like betrayal. All I heard was screaming, endless screaming, so long and hard. At intervals it was silent when she was out of breath, with her mouth wide open, face red and taut, eyes squeezed closed. My ears rang with the high-pitched sound of pain and panic, hers and mine. I held back sobs though my tears leaked; my body was rigid. For the spinal tap, such precision was needed that the team of techs would not allow me to hold her, for safety, so I channeled my distress by gripping Joe's hand, my head leaning on his shoulder.

As midnight came and went, I began to worry about Joe's return to twelve-hour shifts the next day. Then we were informed that Kieran would be admitted for an unknown duration to receive IV antibiotics while cultures grew to discover the cause of infection. Right away I had to make a difficult decision: stay overnight at the hospital or go home. There was an older, heavyset nurse on duty whose body language more than any spoken words assured me she would take care of our baby, and I weighed the needs of

Michael and myself before saying, "I'll come back in the morning." The sureness I felt in this choice had come from a wise place inside that knew I needed to care for myself too, but even so my heart clenched when we returned home to an empty crib.

The next morning, when I entered the room where Kieran lay sleeping in a high metal crib, a nurse was recording something in a file. "Good morning," she said, in a friendly tone. "Kieran did well through the night, the notes say."

"That's good to hear," I managed, nearly consumed with worry, and wishing for Joe's steadying presence, but he was at work.

I tried to project calm. I wanted to be a perfectly capable mother, but my reserves were already spent. Later in the morning, when a different nurse interrupted my feeding of Kieran to check her vitals, I barked, "Can't you see we're in the middle of something here?!"

As the Inner Lost Girl confronted the gritty rigors of motherhood, I felt utterly alone and so aware of being motherless that I explicitly thought, *If my mom were alive, she would be here with me whenever I asked, to trade off with me staying with Kieran or keeping Michael the whole time so I didn't have to worry about him.* It barely crossed my mind to request Ag's assistance. She would be busy with holiday plans, and her organized nature precluded flexibility; her time required advance booking. Not asking saved me the upset of being turned down.

The urine results came in first and confirmed a bladder infection. This good news triggered additional tests that were administered early the next morning when I was not even there. I didn't allow myself to visualize Kieran's likely terror in these unknown scenarios that ultimately identified reflux of urine as the underlying cause of infection. IV antibiotics had begun.

On Thanksgiving morning, I sat in a rocking chair nursing

Kieran, across from the pediatrician from our practice who was making rounds all week. "When can she go home?"

I wanted her to be better and for things to be normal again. The doctor sat back, legs crossed and stroking his beard as though we were old friends having a chat. He had been patient and kind in our interactions thus far.

"Well, the literature says she needs to have the IV for at least five days. You could learn how to manage it at home with a visiting nurse, and then you could leave on Saturday."

"*Yes!* I'll do anything."

The hospital was quiet the rest of the holiday. Joe was off work, so he and Michael did our usual Thanksgiving things with relatives, the knowledge of which consoled me. Kieran's godmother, Joe's sister-in-law, Joni, came by to visit and gave me a break to get something to eat in the cafeteria.

The IV instruction was not a quick demonstration by the bedside, I discovered on Friday morning. I was taken to a conference room for a three-hour session, and there was no comforting nurse on hand to tend to Kieran. Joe was back at work. Being caught unawares forced me out of habitual self-sufficiency. I made several desperate calls to family and friends to come down. Yes, it was the day after Thanksgiving, but I couldn't help feeling hurt that Joe's parents were too busy with his sister's in-laws visiting from out of town. Ag's assistance on anything always had to be arranged well in advance, so I hadn't expected her to come. Still, the refusal stung.

When I got back to Kieran's room from the training, her splotched face and labored breathing told me that she had screamed and cried alone for God knows how long while I was off learning how to operate an IV infusion. Guilt enveloped me and wouldn't let go. Who was I really trying to take care of with this intense need to leave the hospital? She was only five weeks old, and we'd only begun to adjust as a family of four when this traumatic event had occurred. Feeling worse about myself in the aftermath did not help my coping.

My teenaged helper from two doors down had filled in lots of hours with Michael during the hospital stay, and he was fine. Joe was at work when I brought Kieran home, exhausted. Somehow, I got through dinner and bedtime with my active twenty-one-month-old toddler on top of normal newborn care and the administration of IV antibiotics at precise eight-hour intervals. Kieran fussed the entire evening and into the night. She would not go to sleep even with endless nursing. Feeling deranged with fatigue, in desperation at two in the morning, I dialed Joe at the restaurant during his closing duties. However, though he empathized, inexplicably the sound of his voice escalated my emotion.

"I can't do this. It's *too much*! I *caaaaan't*!" I screamed, sobbing. Then I slammed down the phone in helpless rage and didn't answer when he called back. He arrived home an hour later when I had reached the spent phase of my tantrum. He held me as I wept quietly, then gently took Kieran from my arms.

"Go to sleep; I'll take her for a while."

His kindness only made me feel worse. "But you've got work tomorrow. You must be worn out."

"I'll be all right." Then, in the way of things with infants, Kieran immediately dropped off and slept soundly for several hours on Joe's chest.

On Monday, Kieran and I saw our regular pediatrician for IV removal and general check-in. We had only become patients of Dr. Williams over the summer, but I already loved her. About my age, she smiled and laughed a lot. Compared to the hospital, the familiar halls and rooms of her office felt like home. Just ten days earlier, Dr. Williams had given Kieran a glowing report at her one-month visit.

Soon she came bustling into the exam room exclaiming, *"What's* happened to Kieran?" Of course, she'd read the file but asked for my account of the week, her sympathetic nods and almond-shaped eyes like those of a friend. Then she explained that Kieran would take a maintenance drug to prevent infection.

"Here's the prescription, one dose daily. It doesn't taste bad. These things often resolve by themselves. It's totally normal that her sleeping would be off after the upheaval of being in the hospital. Hang in there, Mom, you're doing great. I'll see you next month for her checkup."

Tears of relief filled my eyes as I held Kieran close after the doctor left the room, and I felt a surge of pride that I had survived. Fortunately, Kieran's physical condition did clear up without further incident. If only all challenges were so efficiently handled. For me, the emotional scars from the illness and hospitalization ran deep, compounding the Inner Lost Girl's reactivity.

Chapter Fourteen

Through the long, cold winter of Kieran's infancy, Michael watched Barney videos while I nursed her and changed both their diapers. Our spring awakening began on an early May morning that dawned brisk and clear. Standing at the front door watching for my friend Elizabeth's minivan, I felt exhilarated to have us all fed, dressed, and packed on time. I had become friends with Elizabeth during high school through Bitsy, and we had recently reconnected as stay-at-home mothers. Because her one-year-old daughter loved going to the zoo so much, Elizabeth had been urging me to join them, and today was the day. Joe now worked in the company office and was away for a few days on business, so I had called Elizabeth, anticipating that a diversion would benefit both me and the kids.

I took a moment to catch my breath, surprised to discover how eager I felt for this adventure. Michael sat on the living room floor with a wood puzzle. I had already buckled Kieran into her infant car seat, ensconced in a blanket, alongside Michael's car seat, which I had removed from my Mazda the night before, and our red nylon diaper bag from Lands' End, stuffed with diapers for both kids, burp cloths, snacks, a sippy cup for Michael, and a water bottle for me. A small cooler beside it held our lunch. Grateful for Elizabeth's offer to drive, when she arrived a few minutes later, I loaded our double stroller and bags in the back while she installed the car seats, and we were off.

Elizabeth had been right to rave about the zoo. Two-year-old Michael practically burst with excitement pointing at the animals he was always naming in picture books and whose sounds he could imitate. Sociable and alert without her brother's incessant need to be in motion, Kieran sat mostly content in the stroller; occasionally I lifted her up to see more closely. Elizabeth had the logistics mastered, so our picnic lunch went smoothly, and I purchased a family membership for us on the way out.

This outing evoked the past too, as though long-dormant seeds had been awaiting the proper environment to germinate. When Elizabeth and I and our children stood at the elephants' outdoor area, leaning against the concrete barricade topped with chain-link fencing, all of a sudden, I saw myself at that exact spot as a first grader on a year-end field trip, chaperoned by my mom with my younger brother in tow. Back then, zoo patrons could feed peanuts to the elephants. Our field trip occurred during an emergence of the seventeen-year cicadas that inhabit southwest Ohio, and Tim joined boys in my class who were catching them and trying to scare the girls, but we were unfazed. My mom wore a short-sleeved yellow cotton flowered dress that buttoned up the front and a light jacket, her purse hung over her arm. I saw her amused smile at the antics, though attentive lest Tim or the boys get out of hand. This flash of memory rose from within, brief but vivid like a bright stone found by the ocean's edge. I grabbed for it before a wave could wash it away.

Joseph-Beth Booksellers had opened not far away from our house shortly after Kieran's birth. Its adjacent coffee shop and cushy couches around a fireplace created a library-like ambiance. Out shopping alone one Saturday while Joe watched the kids, I stepped through the double doors and strode to the information desk at the back, prepared to cross a momentous threshold.

I spoke in the firm, confident voice I had used to sound professional when conducting interviews as a journalist. "Do you have *Motherless Daughters* by Hope Edelman?"

The woman came out from behind the counter and led me to the self-help/psychology section, where she found it easily. This groundbreaking book had been published several months earlier, and I had seen an article about it in a magazine. The author had lost her mom at age seventeen, also from breast cancer. After a decade of fruitless searching for resources specific to her situation, she finally decided to create one. Reading the book back at home, I absorbed the content as if quenching the profound thirst of a long desert exile. The title alone named my experience in a way I had never heard before. Filled with personal stories as well as grief research, *Motherless Daughters* kindled my first awareness of other women who shared my experience. It provided context I had never had.

As my days as the mother of two took shape over weeks and months, more recollections of childhood at home with my mom surfaced in the earthy, bodily tasks of tending young children. In memory I saw her changing Tim's diapers, dunking the cloth in the toilet to remove the poop before wringing and putting it in the pail to be laundered later. Caring for our home as a grown-up, I used Comet powdered cleanser to clean the bathtub because I remembered my mom doing so. First, she had dampened the bottom of the tub, then sprinkled the Comet all around, added a bit more water, and with a damp sponge rubbed the powder into a bluish-green, gritty, pasty liquid. She had scrubbed the bottom and sides with the sponge then run the water again to rinse, using the sponge to spread the water around the whole tub. I always loved the color of Comet, the gesture of sprinkling the powder, and even the strong smell. I performed this task like a ritual, enjoying all the sensory associations.

Ordinary actions like zipping my children into windbreakers or washing their hair under the bathtub spigot (while they flailed and fussed as I always had) or tying their shoes could transport me back in time, teasing a nearly forgotten backstory where my mom loved me so, so much. At these moments, savoring the warmth of connection, the enormity of *her* loss took my breath away.

We enrolled Michael in a Montessori preschool when he was three and a half, and I adored his teacher, Yvonne. He was thriving in her classroom's loving environment, engaged with beautiful learning materials, and anchored in routine. At Christmas, I became fixated about her gift, wanting it to reflect my highest values and depth of affection. It was going to be cookies that Michael helped make, presented in little baskets that afterward could be used in the classroom. Then, the last day before break became a snow day, called the night before. Realizing that Michael would *not* deliver these special gifts on time thrust me over a precipice. I exploded with frustration, roaring out at Joe, and stomped upstairs. Michael and Kieran were playing in the living room and didn't pay any attention.

Six months pregnant with our third child, I plopped across the bed in the dark, sobbing into the mattress. The emotional fog was just beginning to lift when Joe entered the room. I heard his staccato footsteps and rapid breathing. Then he unclipped his watch in preparation for bathing Michael and Kieran. The withdrawal of rage's energy left me wrung out like wet laundry. Now a stabbing pain deep in my gut cut off breath. As Joe walked by the bed, I managed to whimper, "I hurt."

His affect shifted immediately, and he sat down next to me, placing his hand on my back. "What?" he asked tenderly, leaning closer.

"I . . . I . . . hurt," I eked out as cleansing tears spilled from my eyes. I sat up, and Joe put his arms around me as I went on thickly, "I'm sorry for blowing up at you. Something's . . . wrong. . . . This isn't about . . . Michael delivering cookies. . . ." More sobs erupted from way down inside, like vomiting. "It's about me . . . not having a mother . . . to make cookies for teacher gifts and . . . and . . . wanting to do that for my child!" I broke down again, and Joe rubbed my back. Finally, I said, more calmly, "Michael doesn't know the difference. He's perfectly fine taking the gift in after Christmas. . . . This is about me."

Joe squeezed me tight as the kids' babble across the hall suddenly turned to shrieks. He left to start their baths while I recovered. Trembling, I wiped my cheeks and eyes and blew my nose, still catching my breath. Then I heaved myself off the bed to join them. The outburst, though draining, had returned my steady self to the present, where I smiled and chattered with wriggling children, wrapped them in towels after Joe lifted them from the tub, and then zipped them into fuzzy sleepers. The day ended with hugs and kisses and saying "I love you" as I tucked blankets around their warm, clean-scented little bodies.

The baskets of cookies were of no consequence anymore. Rather than give stale holiday sweets when school resumed, we bought something I no longer even recall, which Michael cheerfully delivered on January 3. Over the ensuing days, I snatched moments to reflect on that excruciating catharsis. While the kids napped or during interludes of peaceful play, I gently probed the gaping vulnerability that I had guarded against for so long. It was a major step for me, not forward but inward, drawing closer to the Inner Lost Girl.

Chapter Fifteen

At five thirty, nascent fussing from the crib in the room next to ours roused us from slumber, as it did most days. Our third child, a son named Christian, woke repeatedly during the night and rose with the birds. His arrival completed our family in late March 1996, two and a half years after Kieran's birth. Often Joe would fetch him for me and then get dressed while I nursed him. Then Joe would change Christian's diaper and take him downstairs while I slept another forty-five minutes or an hour before Joe left for work. When Michael and Kieran woke up, I would serve their cereal or waffles, pour them juice, and down some toast and coffee myself.

Life had become more intense. Though he slept far less than his older siblings had, Christian was much more sensitive to sounds, textures, and emotions than they had been. When he wanted something, he meant now. If he did not like something, he made it clear, vocally. Christian also was highly affectionate and cuddly, with blond hair and adorable blue eyes, endearing traits that balanced his demanding nature. Now a veteran mother, I approached breastfeeding and infant care with confidence, but more complex family dynamics pressed new buttons for me.

The Art of Reassembly

The typical morning rhythm alternated necessary tasks with nursing the baby, changing his diaper or Kieran's, mediating disputes between Michael and Kieran, and sipping coffee. Christian did not tolerate being left alone for long, so I had to be quick about chores. I learned to do things one-handed, with him held firmly over my forearm, tummy down, a position that seemed to soothe him, and at nearly four and a half, Michael could be relied upon for brief distraction.

"Hey, Michael, Mommy needs to go down and take care of the laundry. Will you talk to Christian for a few minutes?" I had placed the baby on his back in the Pack 'n Play set up in the dining room as a safe interim spot to deposit Christian when needed. Kieran overheard my request and joined Michael by the side of the Pack 'n Play. Sighing, I hoped for the best.

Down at the washer, I heard Michael cooing to Christian and rattling a toy gently. Then Kieran interjected firmly. "No, look, he wants to play with this elephant." Sounds of scuffle, Michael's voice of protest, and beginning fussing sounds from Christian. Then escalation.

"Kieeeran, stop! Mom! She's . . ."

"No, Michael!"

"*Waaaah!*"

Quickly I tossed the last handful of socks in the dryer, slammed the door shut, and pressed the start button. Adrenaline surged as I raced back up to where the scene was unfolding. Then I exploded.

"*Stop!* Kieran, can't you see he doesn't like that in his face? You're going to hurt him. You brat! All I wanted was a few minutes to switch the loads! Can't you just leave him in peace?"

Unrepentant, she gave me a stony stare, her chin jutted out and her eyebrows pinched together, and it was gasoline on a fire.

"*Just go away!* Upstairs! Out of my sight!" My volume grew as my tantrum took hold, the familiar feeling of overwhelm rising within and the plaintive voice whining in my head, *I can't do this. This is too much.* I became a raging mother, venting frustration that my plan for distracting the baby had been disrupted by an almost-three-year-old. My outburst was out of proportion to the incident, and I felt uneasy in the unexpressed awareness that I yelled at Kieran more often and more harshly than I ever rebuked Michael. I detected something irrational in my flare-ups toward her.

Shame prickled as I lifted Christian out of the Pack 'n Play and held him over my right shoulder. *Oh no, he can't be nuzzling my neck again! Didn't I just do this? Sigh.* . . . Shoulders slumped, tears welling, I yielded to the inevitable and carried him upstairs, heading for the rocking chair in his room. On impulse, I changed course and went to sit on the floor in the room with two toddler beds that Michael and Kieran shared.

Kieran sat in her bed, clutching the stuffed clown that she never slept without. A round-faced little girl with short light-brown hair and adorable dimples in her apple cheeks, though no sign of them right then, she had hazel eyes that now just appeared dull gray. Remnants of her tears squeezed my heart as I sank to the floor across from her, leaning against Michael's bed. Without conscious thought, I lifted my pajama top to let Christian latch on.

We sat in silence for a few minutes. As anger's grip loosened, a wave of fatigue washed over me with a softening effect.

"I'm sorry I yelled at you, sweetie," I said softly.

She glared at me, considering.

"Mommy is tired and that makes me cranky. I shouldn't take it out on you. Will you come over here? May I give you a hug?" I could not possibly explain to her about my "issues of loss."

She nodded, climbed out of bed, and snuggled up to my right side by Christian's feet. I wrapped my arm around her sturdy body and kissed the top of her head, whispering, "I'm sorry. I love you."

The spark of personality lit her face once more, and she giggled when Christian pushed his feet against her side.

"Would you like me to read a story?" There were books on the floor over in the corner, and as I switched Christian to the other breast, she grabbed a couple. Eventually he fell asleep, and Kieran moved to the shelf of toys. Rather than risk waking him by setting him down, I stayed in place. I may have dozed myself as she played and Christian slept. Michael joined us, and I basked in their imaginative play with blocks and plastic action figures. The day moved on, outwardly tranquil, but remorse flourished inside.

As the kids grew, my erratic emotional responses remained constant. When disputes arose—over toys, over who was responsible for the playroom mess, over whose turn it was to empty the dishwasher—I could erupt. Too often I would blame or criticize Kieran, followed by an apology and inner self-loathing.

Sometimes during a tirade, I would turn to Joe, chagrined, and say, "My god, I sound like my dad."

"Al's not all wrong!" he would reply with a smile, affirming that, yes, the toys did need picking up, the children should take responsibility, and he shared my frustration. I appreciated his support but could not let myself off the hook so easily. Deep in my bones, I knew that my reactions meant more than normal parenting stress. The irrational escalation that got triggered caused me terrible guilt, and I feared the potential harm I was inflicting, especially on my daughter.

Motherhood's tender moments continued to offer soothing balm as well, an ongoing emotional seesaw. My heart swelled as my kids grew to love the library as much as I always had. We joined a swim club, and they loved swimming too. Besides regular outings to the zoo, we enjoyed museums and parks, on our own and with other moms and kids. In time, Kieran and Christian joined Michael at the Montessori school, and I became a regular lunchroom volunteer. All these activities along with the daily round of domestic mothering tasks forged a link to my mom and the way I had spent my early childhood with her.

To the outer world, I presented competent self-sufficiency because I needed to feel in control. When I hired babysitters, I spelled out the order of the evening, when to have animal cookies or pretzels and which bowls to serve them in, when to put on pajamas and turn out the light. I gave detailed instructions about routine activities like which books to read at bedtime and how far to crack open the door. I issued precautions about wearing bike helmets and defined parameters for outdoor play. I only engaged caregivers if I trusted them to follow my instructions.

Given my history, I also felt it important to teach my children about death, so we took them to visitations and funerals from an early age, passing along the training that I had received from Ag. I never named it aloud, but sheer terror of dying young, as my mom had, lurked behind these death-education efforts, like fire drills for early mother loss. In my thirties, the angst naturally centered on breast cancer as I moved toward the ages of my mom's diagnosis and death. It became imperative to confront this medical risk, especially after my mom's youngest sister, then age fifty-five, was diagnosed with breast cancer.

At the time, I was still breastfeeding Christian, which prevented the logical step of having a screening mammogram. When he transitioned to nursing only at waking and bedtime, my midwife suggested I go ahead and schedule the scan. She thought it would be fine. However, at the testing center, after I answered honestly to all questions on the registration form, including the one about breast-feeding, a technician was summoned from the back. She glanced briefly at the paper and then leveled judgment: "Valid scans cannot be obtained on lactating women! We will not see you today."

Following this rebuke, I slinked away, unsure what to do

next. Breastfeeding was integral to my mothering. Was the risk of future cancer worth upending our bond? That didn't feel quite right, but the expectation of my early death hovered relentlessly. I never knew when it would engulf me like a tornado, threatening removal from the life I loved. One day I shared my worries with another mom at my children's school. She was a nurse, and her reply became a lifeline.

"I know someone else with this kind of family history. She sees a breast specialist once a year, in addition to her regular physical. You could do that and start mammograms when you're ready," she said, and she recommended a doctor.

"Thank you so much!" A plan lent a degree of control, and if one day I found a lump, at least I would already have a doctor.

At my first appointment with Dr. Cornell, this sound rationale could not prevent my trembling in the waiting room. I had traversed the labyrinthine halls of the hospital complex to the office suite as though walking the plank to a death sentence. Posters on the wall advertised wigs, while pamphlets in a rack illustrated how to perform a breast self-exam. Suddenly it all felt too real. What was I doing here? I could not possibly have breast cancer. Yet my mom had confronted the disease at my age. My heart broke to imagine what she must have endured.

An image of my dad flashed through my mind, seated on my twin bed in the room I had shared with my sister, our two brothers standing behind him. I heard again how Dad's voice cracked when he said, "Well, kids, we have an angel in the family."

The memory dissolved as I heard my name called to see the doctor. In the exam room, after I explained my situation, the nurse, Nina, looked straight at me with sorrow in her gray eyes as she said, "Oh, I am sorry. You were so young."

She spoke as though my mom had died weeks ago rather than decades.

"Th-thank . . . you," I stuttered, flustered but also touched by her sensitivity to childhood grief, unexpected in any setting but especially in a clinical one. When reciting my family medical history, I had grown used to the listener's eyes widening at my mom's early death and its cause. Next would come a thorough questioning about other family members while making careful notations in my file, and I would feel like an exotic lab specimen. This time was different.

From the first, Dr. Cornell defied my medical stereotypes. Slender and fit, she was about my age and looked like she had just come from the beach, with tan skin, dark eyes, and blond highlights. I sensed our mutual assessment of one another as we talked. To my great relief, she did not order me to stop breastfeeding and have a mammogram. Nor did she criticize extended breastfeeding, though her blank expression suggested withheld doubt about its necessity. Such restraint earned my trust. She only urged a mammogram in general terms. Unlike all the other health professionals I had ever told my story to, Dr. Cornell seemed unfazed by my mom's premenopausal cancer.

"All women are at risk for breast cancer," she said with a small shrug. "Your aunt was at menopausal age when she was diagnosed. That's very different than your mother, who was young. You may have more risk, but we all need to be vigilant."

From her vantage point, it seemed, I was one woman among many with risk potential, not a uniquely doomed individual. Rather than sweeping me up in fear, her understated manner made me feel grounded.

Continuing in a pragmatic tone, she handed me a brochure on the genetic-testing program at the University of Cincinnati. "I strongly suggest that you pursue this," she said, her chocolate-brown eyes fixed on mine.

Though she had given me a pass on the mammogram for the

time being, I understood that she expected a report back the following year. The concept of genetic breast cancer was familiar to me because of Ag's family, where the gene had been identified.

"Yep," Dr. Cornell said, nodding, when I recounted that situation. "If you have the gene, I wouldn't hesitate to say, 'Lop them off.'"

The trifold paper sat on our living room table for a few weeks before I worked up my nerve to schedule an appointment. The process felt like standing at the entrance of a dark cave, until finally I walked another plank of hallways to the genetics consultation, only to learn that, at this point in time, the test did not produce clear-cut results like cholesterol. Identifying a mutation is like looking for a needle in a haystack, the counselor said. Further, she advised that my aunt was the person to be tested, because her cancer history would focus the search. When the results showed that my aunt did not have the gene, it meant that presumably my mom had not and that neither did I.

This outcome indicated almost nothing new. While it avoided a major surgical intervention, the ambiguity was not reassuring. However, it did affirm my plan for annual assessments with Dr. Cornell. By the next year, Christian weaned, I had a mammogram, and it was totally normal.

"You have great breasts," Dr. Cornell said, characteristically frank as she prodded and pressed my flesh during the subsequent appointment.

"Why, thank you!" I replied, grinning.

Laughing, she said, "I meant the tissue is clear, and they scan well."

In the workshop room, my partner and I sat on the floor facing each other, cross-legged. The sounds of other pairs of our fellow participants receded as I began speaking. The instant this exercise for healing birth memories was introduced, I had known that my painful memory in need of healing concerned Kieran's hospitalization as a five-week-old newborn.

"Tell your partner what happened, in detail. Include as many sensory aspects as you can. As the listener, simply witness the story without any comments or advice," the workshop leader had instructed.

Kieran was nearly seven years old now. Digging into that terrible episode, I could not hide from how bad I felt about her abandoned afternoon while I received IV training. Speaking of it again, even all this time later, caused my hands to tingle with remembered anxiety as my eyes leaked tears. My partner nodded slowly at points, her eyes reflecting empathy.

The next step was to draw an image of our painful experience on a large sheet of paper using chalk pastel crayons. I picked up a black crayon and sketched a stark crib with a stick-figure baby lying in it. Above, I wrote "Waa" and vertical squiggly lines across the page to show the crying. Then I set down the crayon, feeling slightly nauseous as I surveyed my image.

The workshop leader stood to give the next instruction. "Now I invite you to reframe your experience. See if you can give it a new meaning—one that is more positive about yourself. You don't have to adopt the new meaning. Just try to see the moment through a different lens."

I stared at my picture for a bit. Then, seeming to act on its own, my right hand reached for a red crayon and drew a big heart around the whole thing, the crib, the baby, the sounds of crying. A tiny release in my chest, like a slow leak from a tire, shifted my mindset. I did see the moment differently. It was true that I was not with Kieran that afternoon at the hospital to hold and comfort her, but I really loved her the whole time. I did not mean for her to be alone. I did not know it would be that way. I was ushered to the training session without warning. I wanted her to be at home with her family, so I had asked for the IV training. All of it came from love. Tears of healing fell. I had done what I could. Even the best, most loving mothers could not control everything. Life happened.

At home the following week, while the kids were at school, I laid the drawing flat on the dining room table and gazed at it intently, allowing anxiety to be triggered again. I breathed deeply, feeling the red heart encircling the crib, and let its warmth ease the trembling. Then I shifted attention from my baby daughter to myself, the Inner Lost Girl, determined not to flinch or look away from her wounds. Again, I posed the question: How would this look through a more positive lens? Instantly my view expanded to wide-angle, and I saw the Inner Lost Girl from my grown-up perspective, as a mother would. "Ooohhh," I breathed aloud, as love and compassion for that young girl overflowed in hot tears down my cheeks. Now I understood my outbursts at Kieran. When I berated my daughter, I rejected my wounded self, ashamed of her vulnerability. I mentally put my arms around her and held her close. "It's all right. I'm here," I assured her silently.

Three decades after my mom's death and just over ten years since my friend's accident had knocked loose buried grief, I had finally spiraled all the way down to greet the Inner Lost Girl face-to-face. I was thirty-seven, the age my mom had been when she died.

Chapter Sixteen

The traffic light ahead turned yellow, so I started to press the minivan's brakes. It was uncanny how often we were stopped at this intersection on our way to school. Waiting for the light to be green again, I gazed toward the building on my left, just up a small hill, that always sparked a pang of longing. It was a children's grief center, housed in space borrowed from the adjacent church. *I would have loved a program like that as a child*, I thought, for the hundredth time.

A woman in our neighborhood volunteered there and knew the founder. Once when we were walking together, she told me all about how it had opened nearly fifteen years earlier in 1986, just the second one in the country. I became curious about children's grief in general and returned to the large but cozy bookstore where I had purchased *Motherless Daughters*, this time seeking a category rather than a specific title.

I was fortunate to discover *The Grieving Child* by Helen Fitzgerald, another pioneer in the field who got her start when she became widowed at a young age with four children. Reading it felt like I had entered my native country. Yes, children need truthful explanations about death in simple language. They need to express their feelings. Most importantly for me, the book also acknowledged in a whole separate chapter that adults may be working through childhood loss. It might be helpful, it suggested, to educate the children in your life to help them cope with death when it inevitably occurs, a kind of retrospective paying forward of what you would have wanted at their age.

My children needed education about death in the past, I realized. They were unaware that I had a mother who died. I still addressed Ag as Mom, and they called her Grandma. No pictures of my mom or us with her were displayed at my parents' home or ours, although I possessed some. Nothing in my children's immediate realm prompted questions about my parentage, which made initiating the conversation even more awkward. The prospect of introducing the idea that mothers could die at all—along with the fact that their own mom had endured this painful loss—stressed me so much that initially I froze up. I did not want to frighten them or, most of all, to alter their perception of me as a capable, normal mom.

Ultimately, as *The Grieving Child* advised, being forthright with my children seemed preferable to "protecting" them from difficult realities. My journey thus far with the Inner Lost Girl also supported the candid approach. I wanted my children to know the whole story. Our Catholic practice, where November is a time to remember the dead, provided a natural framework to expand their awareness into more delicate territory. The kids were seven, nine, and eleven years old the first time I displayed relatives' pictures on the front-hall credenza for the feasts of All Saints' and All Souls' to kick off the month. I included my mom in a selection that also contained their great-grandparents on both sides.

Trying to sound casual, I presented my mom's picture, a portrait of her on her wedding day. "Now, this is someone you haven't really heard about before. Actually, I had a mom before Grandma.

Her name was Mary Lee, and she died when I was young. So, she's your grandma too."

Christian soon drifted away, but Michael and Kieran kept their eyes trained on my face, rapt. I swallowed the lump in my throat and plunged on.

"Remember Uncle Bill and Aunt Margie, who we see sometimes? Well, Uncle Bill was her twin brother, and Jeanne and Judy, remember, they're my aunts, her younger sisters."

"How old were you?" Kieran asked.

"I was seven," I replied.

"How did she die?" Michael wanted to know.

"Breast cancer," I said. "Then, four years later, Grandpa got married to Ag, your grandma, and then Mark was born. That's why he's so much younger."

I saw the penny drop. A quick shadow sobered Michael's expression. Kieran, eyebrows drawn together in concern, touched my arm lightly and said, "I'm so sad you had a mom that died." A note of anguish lent her words precocious wisdom.

We had already taught them what to say to the bereaved at a funeral visitation, but receiving such expression from her rattled me. I rallied with my standard reply, which seemed age-appropriate in this case.

"Yes, it was hard and sad, but Grandpa and Uncle Mike and my grandparents took care of us. We had each other."

That seemed to settle the subject. After glancing again at the photos, they went off to play outside. I exhaled shakily but still felt satisfied with their introduction to my mom.

On a weekday morning, as we hurried to get out of the house to school and Kieran wasn't ready, I merely sighed without yelling. I stood waiting in the kitchen with my purse and keys after Michael and Christian had gone to the car. No burst of flame ignited an inner fuse. I had grown so accustomed to the Inner Lost Girl's angst impacting my behavior that I didn't immediately notice when it began to recede.

"Don't forget your lunch," I said as Kieran dashed by, "and you'll need a hat. It's cold."

Not that I never lost my temper or had turned into a saint, but now my responses made more sense. They arose more directly from the situation at hand.

Kieran and Christian disliked going on errands. When Michael was almost twelve, they began begging me to let them stay at home with him as the babysitter. Michael was agreeable and had always been steady and responsible, so I began leaving him in charge during the day for short periods. Returning from the grocery store one afternoon, I called into the house, "I'm back!" just as Michael entered the kitchen for a snack. Unprompted, he followed me to the garage to help bring in the bags. I heard Kieran and Christian reading aloud in the family room as I put away the food, and then they both exploded in giggles.

Suddenly a film reel of Ag's Wednesday grocery trips unspooled in my mind, silent footage of me in my school uniform playing outside or in the basement with Mark and then dutifully helping her unload. The contrast slammed me in the chest as those burdened afternoons juxtaposed with my children's innocent ease. In mounting horror, I watched those scenes unfold from the outside, as a forty-year-old adult. When Mark was born, Ag was forty, and I was twelve. Ag was the grown-up then. I was a child. Yes, *I was a child.* Overmaturity had made me feel so much older, but still, I'd been a child. My god.

I didn't share this flashback with Michael, but it brought me up short for a moment. Was I repeating a harmful cycle? No, I realized, after some time to think. The situations were entirely different. Michael, Joe, and I had discussed and agreed that he was ready for babysitting. We were allowing him to grow, not expecting him to assume adult responsibilities.

My parents' number appeared in our caller ID screen on a Sunday, late morning, and I weighed whether to answer as I counted the rings before voicemail kicked in. I finally chose to pick it up to avoid having to call back. My relationship with Ag had settled into a cordial but superficial pattern as we glossed over the tension of Mark's adolescence. We invited my parents over for the kids' birthdays and celebrated holidays together. They faithfully attended dance recitals and plays. Mark's depression had begun to lift during his senior year of high school. Afterward, he attended college locally and continued his informal presence in our family during that time. Now fully independent, he was busy building a successful marketing career and engaged to be married. Happily, he got along well with Ag and Dad now, a repair that evolved over time without my involvement. Still, Ag's phone calls rattled me. As always, they opened with sweet-voiced small talk.

"Hey . . . this is Mom . . . how are you?" she oozed.

"Good, thanks. How are you?" I replied, my body stiff but still managing a loose, friendly voice.

"I'm fine, thanks. The reason I'm calling is that I've got this mirrored tray that was your mother's. I don't need it anymore and thought you might want it."

Was I imagining it, or did her tone hold a tinge of pride at her generosity toward me? I couldn't visualize what she was talking about at all. A mirrored tray? Of course I wanted it if it had belonged to my mom. My insides clenched at the necessity of engaging this conversation at all as she continued, "I'm going out to the shopping center this afternoon and could bring it by then. Will you be home around three?"

"Yes, that will work. Thanks."

Several hours later, she presented me with a flat, rectangular object wrapped inside a gray plastic bag from a local department store. As we stood in our front hall, I removed the tray, edged in thick gold filigree, and she watched, smiling in that saccharine way that always made me cringe inwardly. Letting the bag drop to the floor, I could hardly believe my eyes.

"Oh, yes . . . thanks . . . I think I do remember this," I said carefully. I did not invite her to come into the family room and visit, enduring several minutes of chitchat before closing the door behind her. I watched through the front window until her car began to move away in the drive before exploding to Joe.

"I cannot fucking believe her! She has used this tray to put her ring holder and makeup on for as long as I can remember—so long in fact that *I didn't even realize it belonged to my mom.* It must have been there when they got married, so she just started using it. All these years later—I grew up, moved out, got married—and still she used *my mom's* tray on her dresser. It's only *now* that she 'doesn't need it anymore' so she sees fit to give it to me, and then to act like she's doing *me* some kind of *favor*—she's oh so good to me—to give me this tray that belonged to my dead mom!"

The raging words spent, I let the sobs come, unable to make sense of her actions. I remembered again my mom's white monogrammed towels as gray rags and felt icky. Was Ag being mean or just extremely insensitive? Her dad had died when she was fourteen months old. How could she not understand the value of personal heirlooms?

"I don't think you're overreacting," Joe said, shaking his head. "That was not a nice thing to do."

The following summer, Joe and I and our kids vacationed in Canada. Passports weren't strictly necessary then, but we decided to renew ours and obtain them for the kids anyway. For the first step in the process, I went downtown to the city health department to obtain birth certificates for all five of us. Walking away from the window at the Vital Statistics Department, feeling curious, I sat down on a wooden bench to examine my birth certificate. I wanted to be detached and for it not to matter, but it did.

Joe's and our three children's documents evoked loving, continuous relationships. Mine punched me in the gut. I had never realized how misleading the adoption change really was. Yes, I was born on August 20, 1963, at Good Samaritan Hospital, Cincinnati, Ohio, attended by Dr. Joseph Crotty, but the document's alteration in 1975 was not noted. Instead, the changes fabricated Ag as my actual mother, listing her name in the appropriate box and her age at the time of my birth, twenty-eight, along with her address at the time, which was a convent. The adoption not only erased Mary Lee Wimberg from this historical record, but it fictionalized my origins.

It was too much to deal with. Even before this discovery, my mom was becoming increasingly remote, someone I didn't know or feel connected to. Now in my early forties, my life already surpassed hers in years and experience, dissipating the private bond I had felt with her as a young mother. After we submitted the passport applications, I filed the extra copies of our birth certificates and slammed the file drawer closed. The awareness I tried to hide gnawed at me anyway. As the notion that Ag was not really my mother took deeper root, simple things grew more complicated.

I never knew when an ordinary activity would create adoption distress, like calling a credit card company to confirm a purchase that appeared on my statement. The conversation began with stating who I was, my address, and then the account number. I reached for my monthly statement to provide purchase details but should have realized there would be one more query.

"Now, to verify your identity, please tell me your mother's maiden name."

"Um . . . Cook?"

"Yes, thank you. Now, what can I help you with?"

The purchase was removed easily, but I hung up with mounting awareness that the legal truth felt at least incomplete if not outright false. On a practical level, I was able to resolve the security-question dilemma by choosing straightforward ones such as "What is the city where you were born?" or "What is your father's middle name?" The larger confusion about maternal identity persisted.

Could adoption be reversed? Could I restore my birth certificate? Such thoughts seemed simultaneously daring and absurd, so I felt too shy to voice them even to Joe, much less consult a lawyer. Instead, I began typing "adoption reversal" and "how to change a birth certificate" into my Web browser, over and over, alone at my computer. I found no articles that addressed my specific situation, but the available information suggested that in Ohio adoption was permanent, period.

PART THREE

Chapter Seventeen

Standing before the glass front doors of the eight-unit condominium building where Ag and Dad lived, I paused to collect myself before pressing the button next to their name. They had moved here when our kids were young, not long after Christian's birth. Through the years on our occasional visits, the three of them would jockey over who got to ring the bell. Arriving alone this early June Saturday morning, I pressed the button, my now-teen-aged children no longer concerned with such things anyway. At eighty, Dad had declined significantly from Alzheimer's. I rode the elevator like an actor just before curtain, mentally preparing for the performance.

The door to their unit stood slightly ajar, so I entered after a perfunctory knock, calling "Hello!" as I passed through the foyer, and turned right into the open-plan living and dining room. The compact galley kitchen was on the left, while straight ahead the blinds were raised on the condo's signature view. The picture window and sliding glass door to the balcony spanned the entire front to take full advantage of the building's perch above the Ohio River snaking among soft rolling hills. The view first beckoned in welcome and then mesmerized. To the west, skyscrapers of downtown Cincinnati rose into the clouds as the sun glistened on the water's surface.

Ag and Mark greeted me from the kitchen. Smile fixed in place, I lightly hugged each of them and accepted a glass of water before we settled in the cozy sitting area facing the windows. Dad was napping, Ag said. I sat on the couch against the far wall, Mark took the love seat on my left, and Ag had sunk into one of the two bucket-style chairs across from me. The chairs and love seat were the same ones purchased by my mom decades earlier and reupholstered twice now by Ag to suit her decor. Today it occurred to me that the adoption conversation had taken place while seated on these furnishings too, though in a different house.

Ag had initiated this unusual gathering for the purpose of discussing Dad's status, so she got right to it. "He can't even finish getting dressed without my reminding him and helping. He wanders around the place during the night, opening drawers and doors. I don't think I can leave him alone at all, even to run to the grocery."

I kept my expression blank as anxiety, guilt, and empathy stiffened my shoulders. I wondered where this was headed as she leaned forward, continuing, "Dr. Collins prescribed a new medication when we were there last week, but these changes are all to be expected with the dementia, he said."

In unison, as if choreographed, Ag and Mark swiveled their faces toward mine. Then Mark picked up the narrative, "Peg, the other night she found him opening the door to the balcony at two o'clock! This is really becoming hard on Mom. She can't go on this way."

I noticed her pallor, and though always slender, now she appeared almost gaunt. *Of course.* This was a coordinated message. Mark and his wife were much closer to Ag and Dad than I was. Ag naturally doted on their one-year-old daughter, Shannon, as we all did. Although I understood Mark's bolstering Ag here, resentment still smoldered. *I should have anticipated this scenario. They want—maybe even expect—me to take regular shifts with Dad to give Ag a break. Is she being manipulative? Yes. She is also desperate. But what about me?*

Michael was away at college; Kieran and Christian were both in high school. Though I served on our local village council and often volunteered with the kids' theater troupe, I was also making plans for writing and other projects. Now Ag and Mark wanted to cast me in the Daughter role I had not filled for quite a while, in the story line I had been leaving for some time. Or at least I had thought so.

Inside my head, silent shrieks burst out, *Nooo!* Then inspiration struck. "Certainly, you need help," I said. "It's not good for your health to be so overworked caring for Dad. I'm happy to make some calls. What do you think you need? Couple afternoons a week, maybe some nighttime coverage?"

Ag sat back, blinking several times in rapid succession. "Uh . . . okay, yes, that would be good."

I succeeded at diverting the focus away from my potential availability, and the conversation then shifted to possible home health and other support resources, my first small challenge to the happy ending. In the end, she and I divided the call list. I realized that hiring help likely would suffice only for the short term, but it gave me room to breathe.

The familiar phone number appeared in the Caller ID screen.

"Hello?"

"Peg, this is Mom."

Uh-oh. I detected a tremor in her voice. Had Dad's behavior worsened, or was there a complication with his care?

121

"Oh, hi. . . ."

Plowing over her usual preliminaries, instead she blurted, "My doctor called. There was a tiny speck of blood detected in my urine at my physical. I had it retested, but the blood is still there. She wants me to see a urologist."

Eighteen months had elapsed since what I half-jokingly referred to as "the ambush meeting" at their condo. Our combined efforts at arranging help had created a regular rotation of caregivers, and I did participate on occasion so Ag could get out. However, Dad had grown more erratic, even belligerent at times, which produced periodic distress phone calls to me or one of my siblings. As Ag spoke, I quickly morphed into my case-manager persona, essentially a grown-up version of Responsible Girl who spoke calmly and remained rational.

I asked questions to ascertain that she would have scans prior to the urology appointment and, yes, she did want me to accompany her. We agreed that she would come to my house, and I would drive from here. After we hung up, I marked my calendar for the appointment, sighing. Blood in her urine was a troubling development on this dull winter afternoon. I recognized the case manager as a form of compartmentalization to help me cope, but it required energy to summon and left me drained afterward. I refused to contemplate, even for a second, what might be causing Ag's symptom.

In the wee hours of a Friday night two weeks later, Ag and the caregivers reached their breaking point with Dad and called 911 because he was combative. He spent a few days in the hospital for evaluation and then entered a memory-care facility. His behavior had finally escalated to where he could no longer be at home. By then, Ag was so depleted that she came down with a severe bronchial infection that rendered her almost unable to speak and produced a deep, rattling cough. I had overseen Dad's transition due to her illness, drawing me further into their orbit. Though

I tried to stay at the periphery, I had always known my direct involvement would be required someday.

Ag and Dad had updated their wills and other documents several years prior to the condo meeting, and I had given my signature as trustee and power of attorney. At the time, their end of life had seemed a hazy future prospect. I had neither questioned their expectation that I would care for them in old age nor considered any specifics of what it might entail. Instinctively, during that meeting at the condo, I had resisted getting too involved to preserve my stamina for later, which had now arrived. With Dad in a care facility and Ag's health uncertain, the moment felt like standing at the foot of a towering mountain, my neck craned back trying to view the summit but unable to do so because I was too close to have any perspective. Seeing no other path up or around it, I relied on past patterns of assuming control and caretaking others.

The afternoon that we met for her urology appointment, Ag's cough was much improved but her complexion still looked wan. As we waited for nearly an hour to see the doctor, I attempted to read my library book about a police detective in London, which normally provided pleasant distraction. Today I could not focus as an inner dilemma raged over whether it was rude for me to read when Ag was just sitting there. I stopped and started several times and then placed my marker in the book and closed it.

Finally, we saw Dr. Dodd. Lean of build, probably late fifties, with graying light brown hair and a trim beard, he spoke barely above a whisper, with economy.

"You have a large tumor in your left kidney. It needs to be removed."

Ag recoiled as if from a blow but remained stoic. I inhaled audibly as my gut seized up. *Oh no. Not this.*

He placed the scans on the light board. Ag studied them in detail, hanging on his every word, while I absorbed only the essentials. Tumor diameter: eight centimeters. Likely malignant, only a 5 percent chance that it was not. More detailed scans needed, then surgery to be scheduled.

Cancer of any kind, even the prospect of it, petrified me. I still saw Dr. Cornell every year, along with my mammogram, and held my breath each time until she entered the exam room proclaiming, "You're *fine*." Now I was being called on to accompany someone else—a person with whom I struggled mightily—through this illness.

We walked to the car in silence. Dread of the drive home, of being up close with her and the diagnosis, weighed on me like a boulder. I inserted the key and buckled my seat belt, catching sight of tears on her cheeks, her hands twisted in her lap.

Say something! "Well, that wasn't the news we wanted to hear," I ventured.

She sobbed briefly. *Oh no, what to do?* I reached over, patted her hand for an instant, and then drew back. She began lamenting the possibility of chemotherapy, of which she had extreme anxiety due to her sisters' past experiences.

The scene felt surreal, as though I were an observer, a fleeting perspective that pointed to a coping strategy. *One thing at a time.* I started the car and backed out of the parking space. Like a new driver, performing each step with deliberation, I checked the rearview mirror, held the steering wheel with both hands, accelerated lightly, and flicked on the turn signal to merge onto the road, braking into the turn. Concentrating on these tasks cleared my mind, allowing the case-manager mode to resume.

"Let's not go there just yet. Remember, Dr. Dodd said he thought it could all be contained in the kidney, and your blood work was normal, as was your kidney function."

She settled down over the course of the drive. We hugged briefly at her car. "Talk to you soon," I said as she got in the driver's seat.

Chapter Eighteen

Four months after Ag's first appointment with Dr. Dodd, on a sunny late afternoon in May, my cell phone jingled as I parked at the strip shopping center near our house, about to pop into a small grocery store to fetch a few things for dinner. It was my dad's care facility calling. However, the person speaking was not a member of the floor staff, providing a mundane report, but the director of nursing, Jan. I had barely brought my full attention to the conversation when her words landed like a blow.

"We've been auditing our records, and your dad has fallen twenty-seven times since he's been here. This is beyond what we can accommodate. He needs a different environment. Our model is not safe for him," she said, her tone kind but firm.

Everything seemed to slow except my heart, which raced. "Oh, my god, are you telling me you're throwing him out?"

After holding it together since Ag's diagnosis and Dad's precipitous decline, I could not handle one more thing. Sobs escaped as I leaned my head against the steering wheel. The previous day I had left the house at five thirty in the morning to pick up Ag for surgery to remove her kidney. In the lead-up to the big day, I had revved myself to go, go, go. Like when I was a child preparing dinner on Saturday night, fulfilling duties brought a sense of control and safety. I had remained at the hospital a total of twelve hours to wait through surgery and recovery until Ag was transported to a room. Kieran had brought me lunch about halfway through the nearly six-hour procedure, having just returned home from her spring semester at college.

"How's it going, Mama?" she had greeted me, handing over a Panera bag and settling in the chair next to mine, legs crossed. I did not recall when she began using that endearment, but it melted my heart every time. We had leaned toward each other to speak quietly in the crowded waiting room.

"Not too bad," I had said, pointing to my thermal coffee mug, library book, and writing journal as I savored her nurturing, which I never took for granted. Years earlier, on an afternoon when she was thirteen, while I was blow-drying my hair using a round brush for styling, a maneuver I'd performed hundreds of times, the brush became stuck in hair at the back of my head. Just a couple tugs trying to muscle it out had only tightened the vise, and I'd panicked. "Oh *no*! Help! I can't get this brush out! What am I going to do?" Though alone, I had exclaimed aloud, my breaths coming in gulps of frustration and anxiety. Then Kieran had appeared from downstairs, offering to help. I was desperate enough to hope that a child could rescue me.

"Oh, please, can you do something to get this out? It's stuck!"

I sat on a straight-backed chair while my composed and patient daughter tended to my tangle. Her short puffs of breath on my neck conveyed her absorption as deep soothing enveloped me like a warm blanket. *This is a real mother-daughter relationship.* Despite my grief and imperfections, I had been given this gift, and for the first time I had regarded myself as worthy of it.

Within a brief interval Kieran had extracted the brush, and I'd hugged her in gratitude, speaking to her as I would a friend.

"Thank you so much, sweetie. You're the best. I don't know what I would have done without you."

"You're welcome," she had replied with a big smile.

As she moved through the teen years and into young adulthood, we still tussled regularly, too, and I let loose with periodic rants, whether from simple frustration at ordinary things or in complex reactivity to triggering events. Kieran had learned to assert herself in response. "Mom, that's not fair," she might say. Or "I can see you're upset. Would you like to talk more later?" On occasion, we might both explode and retreat to our corners, but always we returned to the conversation, understanding sought, apologies given, feelings acknowledged. Honesty reigned in our relationship, and I cherished both the periodic clashes and the tender moments.

On this day of Ag's kidney surgery, Kieran had stayed with me an hour or so. Mark had joined me at the hospital shortly before the post-op briefing. Ag had done well throughout, Dr. Dodd reported, and he had removed several lymph nodes for testing. Adrenalin could carry me only so far, and now a day later the brink of exhaustion loomed alongside ongoing care needs. Tomorrow I would bring Ag home from the hospital, and I had been communicating with friends and family to arrange meals and other help for the next few days.

Now Jan's phone call signaled a simultaneous crisis in Dad's situation as well. "I'm sorry," Jan said. "I know this is hard."

"I cannot *even* believe you are doing this right now! This is about the worst timing imaginable."

I raised my head from the steering wheel and stared unseeing out the windshield as grocery customers walked past, allowing an awkward pause until sudden suspicion took root. Jan had been warmly supportive in our dealings to this point. Why would she pile on stress now?

"Did my mother tell you what's been going on with her?"

"She called me last week and said that she would be unavailable for a while and that you would be the primary contact."

"Dear god, I cannot believe her!"

Prior to her surgery, Ag and I had agreed that I would be called first during her recovery, but I had assumed she would explain to the facility the reason why. Her tumor was hardly a state secret!

After I summarized Ag's illness, Jan's remorse was genuine. "I am *so* sorry. I had no idea. Don't even worry about your dad at least until next week. In the meantime, I'll put together a list of possible places, and I'll call them first, to see whether they have a room available. Would that help?"

Now undone by her kindness, more tears flowed, gently this time. "Yes, thank you," I sniffed, "I really appreciate it."

The next day, on the way home from the hospital, Ag and I stopped at the pharmacy, and she waited in the car while I ran in to drop off prescriptions before returning to their condo. I heated soup for her lunch and then drove back to the pharmacy and retrieved the prescriptions while she rested. The news about Dad would wait a few days, I decided. Ag's downstairs neighbor, a dear friend, was coming to bring dinner and stay overnight, so it was the home stretch.

Ag's eyes were brighter after the nap, I noted, though she appeared even thinner after only two days in the hospital. Later, I would send an email updating various relatives and friends, drawing on such observations. In the moment, I ignored the stiffening of my body that marked rising anxiety. Ag seated herself at the dining room table, facing the river view, to sort and read the mail that had accumulated in her absence. I brought her a snack of cheese and crackers and grapes, plus a glass of water and a dose of antibiotic. She talked the entire time, a running monologue about nothing.

Hearing her voice carry through the pass-through window as I loaded the dishwasher, I shuddered from a sickening sense of déjà vu. Suddenly, I was twelve years old again, listening to her chatter on about Mark or her tennis group or housecleaning or dinner or who knows what, with me nodding or asking questions in response. Now mildly nauseous, I felt myself occupying that old Daughter place again, a supporting role in the drama of life where she was the lead. Did I imagine it, or was she loving this old, familiar script? Was that the source of her present contentment?

I finished wiping the counter, wrung out the cloth, and hung it over the faucet. After drying my hands, I walked around to where Ag sat.

"Claire will be here in about an hour. I think you're fine on your own till then, don't you? It's time for me to go home," I said, friendly, but the infinitesimal widening of her eyes told me she'd heard my resolve.

"Uh, yeah . . . that should be fine," she said.

"I'll talk to you tomorrow. Have a good night," I said, cheerful.

Walking across the condo parking lot, I inhaled deeply of the fresh spring air, fragrant from blooming trees in the surrounding yards. I paused by my car with my eyes closed as a cool breeze caressed my arms and face. I trembled a little, like I had made a narrow escape. Joe was chopping vegetables for dinner when I arrived home.

"Please hug me. I'm really drained," I said, enveloped with gratitude for the sanctuary of our life. Later we would eat and laugh around the table with our nearly grown children. I belonged fully in this story. My authentic self was safe here.

"I had an unfortunate call from Jan the other day," I said to Ag, both of us seated at her dining table this time. Sharing the latest development with Dad, I was prepared for her to break down in distress or to pose nitpicky questions that I couldn't answer, or both. Instead, she just looked at me, as though she had not comprehended my words.

"Jan is going to give me places to call this week," I went on, thinking that would spark interest, but she merely nodded and said, "That's good." In her postoperative state, such a bland reaction was understandable, but it was so out of character that it unnerved me.

Because of the time element, I visited all the prospective places on my own while Ag continued recovering at home. Weighing all the options, I chose an older facility that appeared unimpressive on the outside, but inside, the linoleum floors were shiny clean, the air smelled fresh, and sunshine streaming through the large windows created a cheerful atmosphere. The rooms were simple, and it would have to be a double, but something there appealed to me. The monthly fee was considerably lower, and I kept hearing Dad's practical voice in my head, supporting this choice as if he and I alone were making the decision. When Ag accompanied me to the intake meeting, her pressed lips conveyed displeasure as we sat across from the social worker, but she was not positioned to create a different plan.

Dad settled in surprisingly well, but only two weeks after his arrival, in the middle of the afternoon I received a call from the facility informing me that he had gone back to bed after breakfast rather than participate in the daily exercise class that he normally enjoyed. His breathing was "wet," indicating fluid in his lungs. Did we want him taken to the hospital? Knowing his wishes and having discussed this with Ag before, I knew the correct answer was no, but for some reason I choked on the word. I could not say it. The outcome of letting his symptoms proceed without intervention, though unstated, was obvious.

"I'm pretty sure we don't but let me just check with my mom to be absolutely certain. I'll call you back in a few minutes."

Ag said what I was unable to in response to my summary of Dad's condition. "Oh no, remember, we never wanted to put him through that again, all that poking and prodding that they'd do. There's no point."

The process accelerated over the next few hours as the message evolved from "You'd better come before morning if you want to see him" to "You need to come now." We surrounded his bed as he breathed his last. It had happened so quickly, yet in many ways Dad had left us long ago because of the Alzheimer's. I took comfort in the hope that he was finally at peace as logistics took center stage. Still recovering from her kidney surgery only five weeks earlier, Ag needed active support to make the arrangements. I accompanied her to the funeral home the next morning, and we met as a group that afternoon with a parish volunteer to plan the mass. That evening I retreated with my journal and later my laptop to compose a eulogy I would deliver at the funeral. Tears fell as I reflected on Dad's life. Before age forty, he had suffered the loss of two infant daughters, become the father of a blind daughter, and lost his wife to cancer. It had not been easy. He had not been easy.

The following day, Mark took Ag to the required meeting at the cemetery while I handled tasks for the reception to be held at our house after the burial. The funeral director kept bothering us about pictures for a slideshow video to play in a continuous loop at the visitation, but that detail became one too many for me. Mark's wife, Laura, wanted to help and could easily scan photos, but still I resisted, dismissing the idea as unimportant. Laura persisted and made a special trip over to our house to pick up specific pictures while Mark and Ag were at the cemetery. Standing in our front hall, I suddenly heard myself apologizing for being so cranky.

"It's just . . . it's just . . . this feels really hard." Tears clogged my throat. "Ag and Dad bought their own double plot at the cemetery a while ago. I've known this for a long time, but just now it's painful. My mom is already buried in a double plot there, but Dad and Ag will be buried together in a different section!" This last came out in a wail.

Compassion crossed Laura's face as tears filled the corners of her eyes too. "I am so sorry. I had no idea. That has got to hurt." Then she hugged me.

The slideshow immediately ceased to be an issue. "Here are some pictures," I said, turning to pick up the stack I had placed on the hall table. "Thanks for doing this."

"I pulled some of ours too. I am happy to do it," she said, and I could hear her sincerity.

For print photos, everyone had concurred with my suggestion that we enlarge several key images of Dad to display on easels at the visitation rather than deal with making collage posters. Time was of the essence, so without consultation I chose which images to enlarge. Deliberating only a moment, I included one of Dad and my mom beaming with youthful innocence and optimism at their 1955 wedding. It felt rather daring, but the past few months of caregiving had boosted my confidence. I felt connected to Dad in a way I had not for a long time. His first marriage was a milestone of his life, I rationalized, to counter the reflexive fear of Ag's censorious marble eyes.

I also selected one of Dad and Ag in the glow of midlife courtship during the fashionable 1970s, with Dad sporting a red-and-blue-striped blazer. At the funeral home, this image elicited quite a few hoots and several admiring queries as to whether we still possessed the jacket. My mom's relatives smiled about the Mary Lee and Al wedding photo in a pleased way I hadn't observed before, as though something in them had been salved too. Friends of all ages remarked on its sweetness, as though its presence were quite natural and expected. I did not notice Ag's reaction.

At the mass, I spoke about Dad's sense of humor and friendships as well as his resilience in the face of many sorrows. However, the pastor provided the most noteworthy moment. A longtime friend of Ag's, he evoked the posters from the evening before to remark on my dad's good fortune to have had two such wonderful wives. Tim and I looked at each other in astonishment and afterward joked in private, "Didn't he know you're not allowed to talk about Mary Lee?" Ag never mentioned the homily or the posters to me, then or later, and I did not broach the subject either.

Chapter Nineteen

In the aftermath of Dad's death, I gritted my teeth through a flurry of new excursions with Ag to their attorney, to their investment advisor, and to banks, to settle his estate and update paperwork, fulfilling the role I had accepted by signing their documents years earlier. I occupied the assistant position once more, rather than leading. Yet Ag's mental acuity was not up to her previous sharpness, so I had to remind her repeatedly what forms were what and reiterate decisions that had been made, interactions requiring a level of diplomacy that I sometimes failed to achieve, resulting in terse exchanges between us.

The surgeon had referred her to an oncologist, Dr. Lowell, and Ag responded well to his talkative, outgoing style. As he examined scans and explained at length the variations of kidney cancer, which was slow growing, and its multiple treatments, I began to understand that cancer had many facets. It was not the monolithic monster that altered my childhood irrevocably. My body relaxed into the molded plastic chair just a bit.

The disease had not been contained in Ag's left kidney, however. She had three small growths in her pelvis and abdomen, but Ag remained opposed to treatment despite his assurances that it was not chemotherapy. I listened to their back-and-forth a bit and then interjected, "She *is* seventy-eight."

He paused, reassessing. "Well, yes." Turning back to Ag, he said, "I keep forgetting! You look much younger. Yes, at seventy-eight any impact on quality of life would be undesirable. I see that. Okay, I want you to be rescanned and to come back in three months."

Ag exhaled and said, "Well, that's a relief."

By the end of the summer, she had resumed daily walks, dinner-and-movie nights out with women friends, and spending Saturday mornings with Mark and Laura's daughter, Shannon. Every three to six months we met at Dr. Lowell's office. On some visits the growths were larger but still small, and a couple times they had shrunk. Every now and again he would mention treatment and then backtrack to reaffirm the current approach, given her age and asymptomatic status.

Mark started joining us for these late-afternoon appointments. Though our threesome in the exam room evoked uncomfortable memories for me of our earlier triangle, soon I realized that his presence had nothing to do with the past. He simply cared about his mom. Ag relaxed more in his company as well, so I could too.

Through this interlude of intermittent oncology appointments, my mindset grew increasingly grounded in present experience rather than in amorphous fear. Cancer could be a winding journey, I was learning, not exclusively a straight-downward dive. This perspective allowed me to lighten up my case-manager role. By now all three of my children had departed the nest for college and beyond, which offered me time and freedom for new pursuits, and I took full advantage.

On an October Saturday morning, I entered a high-ceilinged meeting room clutching a large coffee and wearing a fixed smile. I had no idea what to expect from this Healing Touch Level One workshop that I had signed up for on a whim, to satisfy longstanding curiosity.

In a basic sense, I understood that Healing Touch helped people recover from illness or after surgery. The instructor, Mary, was a friend who had been practicing it for twenty years. Brian, a former colleague of my husband's, offered Healing Touch twice a month at the food pantry where I volunteered, and his gentle but persistent encouragement had led to my presence today.

Mary sounded a chime to call the group to order, and thirty of us settled in our chairs, arranged in a large circle facing one another. Mary stood to begin. "First, I invite you just to experience energy. Rub your palms together, back and forth for a bit," Mary said, demonstrating. We remarked on the tingling sensation, and she said, "That's energy."

"Now, hold your palms facing each other about a foot apart. Gently move your hands closer to each other and farther apart. What do you notice?"

Hmm. This is interesting. I could sense an edge as I moved my hands closer. There was pressure or shape, almost like holding a ball between my hands. My morning sluggishness evaporated, and I sat up straighter, my gaze now focused on Mary.

"That's energy," she said, smiling. "Probably you've been aware of it all your life. Think about the words we use to describe how we feel—drained, pumped, wiped out. These are energy words. Learning and practicing Healing Touch means being more intentional about it."

We worked in pairs to scan our partner's energy field by moving our hands from head to toe, several inches away from the body, as the other person sat in a chair.

"Whatever you're able to sense is fine," Mary said. "Most people become more sensitive with practice, but you can still do Healing Touch even if you don't."

By six o'clock, Mary had taught us about the body's energy centers, called chakras, as well as several Healing Touch techniques that brought deep relaxation, and I was hooked. Energy seemed both palpable and cosmic at the same time, which fascinated me. Within a few months, I joined the Healing Touch volunteer team at the food pantry, offering brief sessions to clients during their wait to shop for groceries. As the pantry hubbub swirled around us, I rested my hands on the shoulders of the person seated in the chair before me, centered and silent. In that stillness, time halted and roles dissolved, if only for a short while.

In the middle of the bustling library, I sat alone at a round table with four chairs, while people tapped away at the computers along the wall behind me. When my mom was alive, she brought us to this library branch regularly. Most memorably, this was the library where I had obtained my first library card, after she helped me practice signing my name in cursive for the application.

I seldom traversed this neighborhood that's only twenty minutes from our home, but an unseen something had pulled me here like a magnet. Since Dad's death, childhood memories and associations emerged more often, with greater clarity, and I savored them. Approaching the library entrance, I had admired the distinctive rectangular pillars beneath the flat portico, made of ordinary cement accented with decorative stones in shades of brown and gray. Before entering through the double glass doors, I'd run my fingers over their bumpy surface and looked up to appreciate the curved arches, smiling with satisfaction that I'd heeded the impulse to come here.

A historical marker by the side of the parking lot noted that the land occupied by this library branch was originally part of a farm whose owner fought for the Union and donated the land for a rest home for Black soldiers of the Civil War. The library was built on the site in 1966, making it still rather new when I applied for my first library card.

On this return visit, once inside I browsed the books, selected a few mysteries, and settled at the table for a while to write in my journal and soak up the atmosphere. Two women waited at the check-out desk. At nearby tables, patrons sat reading the newspaper or books, while several others were filling out forms. I felt welcome but not particularly noticed, which suited my purpose.

Afterward, driving west a few miles farther, I arrived at Little Flower Parish, where I had attended school from second grade till our move in the middle of sixth grade. While the parish continues, the school has merged with several other parishes and relocated elsewhere. The parking lot sat mostly empty, the large school windows dark. I parked briefly on the side street alongside the deserted playground, feeling conspicuous as an outsider. A depressed air hung over the neighborhood that I recollected as vibrant. Cracks and potholes marred the once-pristine streets.

The thought *This is where I was motherless* came unbidden, stated quietly inside. I stayed in the car and snapped a couple of photos with my phone before returning home. Over the next several days, I felt activated somehow by Little Flower, as if a Geiger counter were buzzing. The pictures I had taken of the parking lot depicted nothing but blacktop and a couple of cars, but still they conjured grade school recess. I saw myself wearing the red-and-green-plaid uniform, probably my red cardigan or maybe a windbreaker or both. What was it about Little Flower School that dampened my palms and set my pulse racing?

Chapter Twenty

In the compartment of my life where Ag's health resided, for two years our recurring oncology appointments became a deceptively reliable routine, as if they would always go on in the same manner. Then, just before the second anniversary of Dad's death, Ag's regular doctor sent her to the emergency room because of sharp pain in her upper back. It might have been a heart attack but turned out to be inflammation. I wondered if this eruption of symptoms signaled the inevitable rough weather system to come, a question I kept to myself. That summer she was hospitalized twice and took a lengthy regimen of steroids.

In early August, Ag called one morning after I had eaten breakfast to ask me to meet her at Dr. Kane's, her regular doctor. In a thin, barely audible voice, she said, "I fell in the hall and my back really hurts. I'm using a walker to get around."

"Um, if you can hardly walk, how are you going to drive? I'll pick you up at ten thirty," I said, my voice gruff with concern about what this new development boded and irritation at this intrusion on my plan for the day.

"Okay, yeah, thanks."

She was not waiting behind the glass doors when I pulled up, which was troubling, so I called her landline. "I'll be right down," she panted. *Why does she sound out of breath?* As she came into view, I got out of the minivan to assist with the walker. She grimaced silently getting in and out of the front seat, her face ashen. Realizing the extent of her pain, my touchy mood softened. Later, as we rode from the doctor's to get an X-ray following another agonizing struggle into the vehicle, reality hit full force: In her present state, she could not possibly manage on her own. I recognized this as a new threshold, after which my authority would necessarily increase and her control would have to loosen.

"You need some help for a while. I'm going to call the agency that Melissa told me about," I announced. Her niece had provided information back at the time of the surgery, but it hadn't been needed. The agency had cared for her mom, Ag's sister. "Remember, Aunt Claire liked them a lot."

Ag's lack of resistance spoke volumes. Her acquiescence lasted about a month until she was moving about more confidently again and began agitating to drive. Physical therapy had restored her ability to handle daily living tasks, but a subtle frailty of body and mind became the new normal. I now felt the need to remind her of appointments the night before and verify that her bills were paid. Mark checked on her more regularly too. Often on the weekend, they would bring over dinner, or Laura would do her nails. His bond with Ag led him to provide emotional support beyond my capabilities, and I was grateful. Mark and I conferred on the phone at least weekly.

At a follow-up appointment, Dr. Kane caught my slight head shake when Ag inquired about driving again, then shifted smoothly into, "Why don't you take the driver assessment over at Drake Hospital? I would like you to do that before you start driving again. Then we can all feel comfortable about it since we don't really know for sure why you fell."

Thus, ferrying Ag to two separate three-hour sessions landed on my calendar. Though it had been at my instigation, my insides seized up at the time involved. The testing location was close to my house, but I had to drive an extra forty-five-minute round trip to transport Ag, in addition to waiting during the test. She got through the first session, and the second one was set for a Monday in mid-October two weeks later. The day before, Mark called to report Ag's wrists and knee were swollen and painful with inflammation.

"I'm already taking her to that driving thing tomorrow." I reminded him, then continued, "I guess we'll need to call Dr. Kane instead." I girded myself against prickles of anxiety. I just could not go there. I had to get through the next twenty-four hours at least.

After dinner, when Ag called to confirm the next day's revised plan, her voice was so weak that I had to ask her to speak up. Our course of action made sense, but bottled-up nerves vibrated through my body all evening and into the night. I lay awake in the dark, pummeled by incessant thoughts. *How long will I have to spend with her? Will we end up in the emergency room for admittance to the hospital? Or for tests in addition to the doctor appointment?* Now eighty, this vulnerable Ag was harder for me to deal with than the controlling one or even the unkind one. I did not want her to need me, and I didn't want to be with her in that way. I required intact barriers. Ag and her cancer had to stay where I had slotted them, but they were threatening to overtake my whole life. At least, that's how it felt. I could not handle being on call like this, responding at a moment's notice with a completely different plan for my day, being pulled deeper and deeper into the belly of the cancer beast.

Not for the first time, it occurred to me that I could resign as Ag's power of attorney and let Mark take over. I was not legally bound to perform these duties. Even while mentally forming the words *I won't do this anymore*, I quivered. To relinquish the role of Ag's Daughter seemed impossible; though uncomfortable, particularly right now, I had lived this "new" story for so long that it was an indelible part of me. The resulting loss of control if I were to disengage also dogged me. Would that prove more challenging than the status quo?

Well past midnight, trembling, I woke Joe.

"I can't stop thinking about tomorrow. I have no way of knowing how the day will go. If we have to go to the hospital, it'll never end. I can't take much more. It's just *too much*! I can't do it! I just *can't!*" I sobbed, repeating with building intensity, as the Inner Lost Girl reaction rose to the surface.

Joe patted my shoulder and said soothingly, "It's all okay. It's going to be fine."

I could tell he was unsure what to do, even after witnessing my emotions for almost twenty-five years. *There's no guarantee it will be okay. It could be a nightmare! In fact, it likely will be!* Ready to launch a blaming blast, I heard a gentle invitation to nurture the lost girl who still resided within.

"Issues of loss will always be significant for you," Dr. Jackson had said long ago.

Ask for what you need, said a wise voice inside now.

Considering eldercare's enormity, my deep-seated fear of cancer, and my profound ambivalence toward Ag, what did I need that Joe could provide right then? Something quite basic, I discovered.

"Would you please . . . hold me like I'm a child who is upset? Pretend I'm a kid and comfort me that way." My voice was nearly a whimper.

"Ohh . . . ," he breathed, and with the firm assurance the lost girl craved, he held me against his chest, cradling my head with his palm, and rocked me gently as I cried and cried, releasing all the pent-up fear, stress, and frustration.

The next day, Ag and I listened to an associate of Dr. Kane's hypothesize that her continued issues resulted from the long course of steroids she had taken. Exhausted from poor sleep, but with the mental and emotional clarity that follows cathartic crying, I finally disclosed what I had kept buried for months.

"I'm not buying that explanation. She's been off the steroids for almost eight weeks, and the symptoms are getting worse. Other than the cancer, she's been incredibly healthy all her life until this past June. Since then, it's been one thing after another. Doesn't it make sense that cancer is causing the inflammation? *That* needs to be investigated, in my opinion."

I rested my case with a nod and stared at him, unwavering, as Ag regarded me wide-eyed. The doctor met my gaze, then glanced down before saying reluctantly, "Dr. Kane is on vacation for another week. I'll review your whole file and consult with Dr. Lowell."

"Thank you," I said.

As the autumn wore on and Ag's state of health grew less predictable, I began to rely on writing more intentionally as a coping mechanism. Most mornings, I off-loaded thoughts and emotions, sometimes even ranted, into my journal. Though I kept up the capable caregiving role, on the page I revealed my full self. It was safe.

Eventually it was agreed that Ag would try an oral cancer drug, starting right after Christmas so that she could enjoy the holiday without concern for side effects. However, within a short interval she experienced fatigue and increasing mental confusion. In early January, Tim arrived at the condo to take Ag for scans, only to find her still in her pajamas at two in the afternoon and unable to focus. He got her to the appointment and then called to raise an alarm.

"Oh wow," I said. "That's definitely outside her norm."

After my middle-of-the-night meltdown in October, I asked for more help from Tim and Mark, which they willingly gave.

Though unspoken, I think we all realized Ag's worsening state and the accompanying need to spread around the work of her care.

She had a fever, but we decided to manage the weekend until her doctor appointment on Monday. Mark volunteered to spend that night with her. I would go over the next morning and contact others to fill in as needed through the weekend. Privately, I anticipated contacting the agency again. I had drawn a mental line at hands-on care and intended to keep this shift brief.

Mark and I chatted over coffee, and he left before ten o'clock. Ag slept till noon, awakening with a start but hardly able to talk or move, her skin warm to the touch. She stood with effort but then just stared vacantly. Several times I said, "Ready to go to the bathroom?" She answered with unintelligible syllables but no movement of her feet. Finally, I held her by the arm and gently guided her with my other arm circling her waist. Like a robot, with empty eyes and rote movements, she used the toilet herself. Then she just looked up at me, and I realized she could not get up. One track in my brain reminded me, *She's got an infection. She's possibly dehydrated*, but the dominant part clamored, *OMG, OMG!* I called Mark to ask how he had had handled this situation.

"Do you want me to come over?"

"Yes, please."

In less than ten minutes, his tall, thin frame filled the bathroom. At six foot seven, what he could easily do to assist her someone of my five-foot-three height could not manage. Speaking as if to his little daughter, he placed Ag's hands on his shoulders and lifted as she held on. Then he pulled up her underwear and pajama bottoms and moved her back to the bed slowly, again with pauses of standing still and garbled speech.

Nearly eight hours later, the three of us huddled in room A22 of the ER. Ag had been officially admitted, a stroke ruled out, blood drawn, and we awaited a room with no time estimate on its availability. Two bags of intravenous fluids had calmed her spirit and cleared her mind. We wanted to feel that Ag was settled in a real room before leaving, though we were told that people often occupied ER cubicles for extended periods. Mark and I were both very tired. I had already called Joe to cancel our plans to attend a concert that evening.

A bit later, another nurse came in and introduced herself as Carly, a friend of our niece Leah's, also a nurse. As we all chatted about their prior working together, Carly stood on the right side of Ag's bed, and Mark and I sat in chairs on the left. Then Ag turned to look up at Carly and said in a singsong voice like a child, "I'm to be left here alone, and I don't like that."

What? Why express this to a stranger who was not even her assigned nurse? Was she genuinely afraid or being manipulative? Both? Or simply confused? I couldn't tell, but I noticed the lack of boiling rage or even irritation in my response. I said, "Mom, that's a concern to discuss with your family members." She just looked at me, her expression blank.

Carly placed a hand on Ag's arm and asked, "Are you scared?"

I expected tears, but Ag only nodded. This exchange altered my view, like rotating a kaleidoscope. In Ag's expression of fear, I heard her wanting what I had longed for when Kieran was hospitalized years earlier as a newborn—an unconditional caring presence, willing to go any distance. Ag desired something from me that she had not given. Meanwhile, though not to her liking, right now she was safe and cared for in important ways not available at home on her own or even with us in attendance there, I realized, in a bed with sides, with a call button to summon someone with a bedpan if necessary, being hydrated with IV fluids.

I said softly to Mark, "I need to go home. I need a break." He agreed and said, "We'll tuck her in for the night and say we're going home to bed too."

A few minutes later, the shift change brought a new nurse who served Ag a turkey sandwich and ginger ale, gave us her direct phone number, and removed the finished IV bag and some of the monitoring devices. Her warmth and attention to detail created confidence that Ag would not get lost in a no-man's-land between the ER and a regular room.

The next day, I wrote in my journal:

Driving home alone on the dark, smooth highway, scenes of the day passed through my mind. For the first time, I appreciated Mark as a kind and generous adult rather than a baby brother. When I was stressed out because Ag couldn't get up off the toilet, he was there for me. I also saw myself more appreciatively. Though all the old tensions in my relationship with Ag have weighed heavily on me since the start of this eldercare odyssey, I've still been effective in my role. I feel proud of my strength and wisdom, making decisions and arranging resources with Ag's best interest in mind. Just as importantly, if not more so, I've begun to notice my own needs too and honor them without apology.

Chapter Twenty-One

Ag entered a rehab facility after five days in the hospital. She gained weight and recovered mobility with a walker, though cognitively she remained prone to confusion and struggled with finding words to express herself. I half-heartedly suggested she move into the residential section of the facility, but Ag's sole focus was going home, which she did a month later with a regimen of continued therapies and caregivers that allowed her some time on her own.

On a Friday afternoon during the interval between caregiver shifts, I stopped in at the condo to check on Ag's medicine dispensing and the mail. I had told her not to worry if she was napping, that I would use my key. I found her sound asleep. My tasks took less time than anticipated, so I sat in the study at the computer table for a bit, daydreaming, gazing at the open shelves of knickknacks and books on the opposite wall.

Slightly bored, contemplating whether to leave or wait a while longer to see if she woke, I was drawn to the photo albums on the left side. Reaching toward the thick burgundy-and-brown-vinyl-covered albums that documented our life since my dad and Ag's marriage in 1974, I noticed a smaller, slim volume tucked among them. Cream-colored but perhaps once white, it was clearly of much older vintage. My file-cabinet forays as a kid had never uncovered this little book. I had not seen it before. Puzzled, I pulled it out and read "Wedding Gifts" imprinted in gold letters on the cover, intuiting immediately that I had uncovered a relic from my parents' wedding in 1955. A sticker on the inside front page identified a local jewelry and china store; perhaps these books were given to all brides who registered there. The next page said "Bride's Book" in the center, and, sure enough, the following slightly yellow pages bore Mary Lee's compact, even script.

I didn't realize I was holding my breath until a few more pages in when I exhaled explosively at the sight of her sole notation on the page headed "Date of Engagement"—"December 25, 1953." *Wow. Just wow. How sweet!* I had never even thought to wonder about my parents' engagement story. They became engaged at Christmas nearly two full years before their actual wedding, probably because my dad was in the army. *My mother was only twenty years old!*

Abruptly recalling where I was, I closed the book. I had known instantly upon holding it in my hands that I would take it with me, claim it as my own discovery. Stepping lightly, I hurried to the living room and slid it into the manila file folder I had brought, beneath the jottings from Ag's recent doctor visit. Then I wrote Ag a brief note, put on my coat, gathered my things, and tiptoed out, closing the door silently behind me.

At a nearby coffee shop, large cup of mint tea in hand, I made a little ceremony of seating myself at a small window table and arranging the book in front of me, even took a photo before opening it at the beginning to turn each page one by one. I felt curiously calm, eager but not giddy, as if I were an actual anthropologist examining a new find. *What is here? What will I learn about the owner of this book and the time of the event it references?*

I returned to the engagement section. Uncle Bud and Aunt

Catherine (whoever they were) sent a "Message of Felicitation," the only one recorded under this heading. Several engagement gifts were listed on a subsequent page. The entry for Jane Wimberg, her cousin and maid of honor, saying she gave "guest towels with monogram" brought a momentary catch to my throat before I continued turning pages. A listing of all the showers and parties and their hosts and locations and type came next. Bar shower, cocktails, personal shower, and more. I recognized several names of the hosts, people who remained my parents' friends throughout my life and even into Ag's and Dad's marriage.

Next, there were pages and pages recording wedding gifts received, predominantly place settings of china and silver and crystal glassware, silver trays and serving dishes, as well as practical items like mixing bowls, a roasting pan, a toaster, TV trays, sheets, pillows, and—a sign of the time period—ash trays. Check marks in the far-right column indicated an acknowledgement had been sent.

For several days following this remarkable discovery, I opened the book again and again to ponder and savor it. I doubted Ag would notice the wedding book's absence now, and even if she did, so what? Had Dad known it was there? Had he taken part in the decision to retain it and place it on that shelf? Though I would never know for sure, I felt grateful, realizing how easily the book could have been pitched at any point during the preceding decades.

"She looks gray, and her forehead is warm to the touch. Plus, she has no appetite today," said Ag's caregiver Allie, my favorite.

I had just stopped by for my usual check-in on this mid-March day. We made a quick call to Dr. Kane, who recommended going to the ER. When we resisted because Ag's symptoms were mild and she did not want all that upheaval, Dr. Kane allowed a long pause before she replied gently, "If you really don't want treatment, then maybe it's time to think about hospice."

"Oh . . . that's a good point," I said. "Let me talk to Ag about it."

I pressed the off button, looked right at Ag, then plunged on without stopping to think. "So, do you want to go to the hospital for this fever? We could wait and see how you do tonight. Or, if you think you really don't want to go to the hospital anymore, then we could call in hospice. It's up to you."

"Yes, let's call hospice," she said without hesitation, sounding tired but clear. "I would like that. I just want to be here, at home."

"I understand. I think it makes sense," I replied, experiencing the exchange almost as a dream. Had we just made such a major decision so simply?

Engaging hospice only took two phone calls. Speaking with Dr. Lowell's assistant, I considered which doctor should continue following Ag's case. My heart was with Dr. Kane, who had been Ag's physician for nearly two decades, but keeping the oncologist involved was more logical. Over the next few days, I attended the intake meeting at the condo, and a chaplain visited Ag, followed by the nurse, Audrey, who would check on her once a week to start and then more often as needed.

Audrey would take over the setting up of medicine dosages for each week. At any sign of concern, such as nausea or increased pain, Ag or whoever was with her could call the main hospice number for a consultation. As the mantle of duties began to lift, my shoulders lowered, and I breathed easier, feeling less alone. Over the following weeks, though, increasingly I felt exposed without the veneer of required tasks. There were no more tests or doctor appointments. Besides bill-paying, my role consisted merely of phone conversations with Audrey. Managing Ag's pain was her top priority, and she worried that Ag's stoicism precluded her seeking comfort. As the spring unfolded, Audrey waited for Ag to request stronger medicine.

"She needs to make the choice for herself, not because we persuaded her in any way," Audrey said.

Ag finally asked for more meds when back pain became too much for her, and Audrey brought the pills to the condo that very afternoon.

"She likely will be more confused, sleep more. If you have anything you want to say, I'd suggest seeing her this weekend," Audrey advised, sounding almost hinting.

I ignored this overture. It churned me up inside, but I disregarded that too.

Several days later, Ag contacted Audrey again because her back still hurt and she hadn't slept for two nights. It was the weekend, so another nurse came and doubled the dosage. On Monday, Audrey checked in and discussed longer-acting meds.

"I'll stop by again today to see how it's going. I want to be out in front of this, make sure the pain management is adequate. If we need to go to morphine, it will take a couple of days to implement," she reported to me on the phone.

My insides lurched, like heading closer and closer to the top of the roller coaster but not knowing for sure when the downward *whoosh* would occur.

In late May, Audrey observed obliquely that Ag is "having a lot of thoughts about her life." Then, she addressed head-on the topic I wanted to avoid as the final threshold drew near: "Is there anything you need to say to her?"

"*No*, there isn't!" I responded, and I thought, *Please, don't push me to open up in ways that I don't want to.* In Ag's emaciated, confused condition, I could not imagine speaking the enormity of things that I might want to say, if I could even find words to articulate them.

I managed to reply, "Our relationship is difficult for me. I don't want to be vulnerable with her. There's just too much water under the bridge at this point."

"You don't have to apologize for your feelings. They just are what they are," Audrey said, reassuring.

"I feel satisfaction at arranging for her care, but I must keep her at arm's length. I'm truly glad that she's able to be at home as she wishes." I spoke quickly, as if trying to convince someone. Myself, or Audrey?

"Whatever you say or don't say, it's always your choice. Just like whatever Ag chooses to say or not say is up to her. You don't have to do anything for her to make that happen." After a pause, Audrey added, "I've said to Ag multiple times, 'Peg takes good care of you.'"

Hmm . . . why would Audrey do that? Suspecting a subtext, I responded from gut instinct, the words unbidden. "Do you think unfinished business with her stepchildren is affecting her?"

"Yes," Audrey said.

Having no idea what to do with that, I said, "Oh, okay. That's interesting. Thanks. I'm sure we'll talk again soon. Bye."

Over dinner, I shared Audrey's insight with Joe. "I find it fascinating, especially if Ag would initiate a conversation with me, but I can't see myself saying anything to her."

Though I did nothing openly about Ag's potential unfinished business, I attended to some of my own by searching adoption key words again. No new legal insights turned up, but I came across a riveting blog by female adoptees called *Lost Daughters*. The name resonated strongly for me, as did some of the themes in their posts. Uncertainty about who I am. Searching for answers to unarticulated questions. Though my circumstances differed in many respects from the adoptee writers, it was good to feel less alone in my yearning.

Chapter Twenty-Two

A letter came to the condo announcing Dr. Kane's retirement at the end of May. Ag showed it to me, and I realized with sad relief that we had no need to arrange to meet the new doctor or attend an orientation session. Ag never mentioned it again, but I remembered the date as the month wore on. On the second-to-last day, I penned a note thanking Dr. Kane for her years of relationship with Ag, especially during the cancer. Visits to her office had been a refuge, I said, like conversing with a friend. I dropped it off with a small box of chocolates. Though not a necessary gesture on my part, an unmistakable sense of duty impelled me to carry out this social nicety on Ag's behalf. She would have marked the occasion somehow had she been well, and I had learned such customs from her.

On that same afternoon, I stopped by the condo to write a monthly check to Allie, her caregiver. Ag was in the bathroom.

"She's been extremely confused today," Allie said, with a slight shake of her head. We sat at the dining room table while I wrote the check and reviewed some mail. "She could not carry on a conversation or give a straight answer about her pain level."

The Art of Reassembly

My chest tightened at this litany. Again, I sensed the roller coaster cranking up to the unknown peak and braced myself for the *whoosh* of descent.

At the dining room table while Allie checked on Ag, my mind involuntarily veered toward the next steps, envisioning the funeral, then the dispersal of belongings. Fired by the wedding-book discovery, I imagined myself claiming the china, crystal, and silver that to me still belonged to my mom, until a sudden worry struck. *Surely it's all still here?* I tiptoed over to the buffet and carefully opened the doors in search of the china. Both side compartments were stuffed with silver bowls and trays in tissue or plastic. The center held drawers for linens so it couldn't be there. *Hmm. Oh, yes, the corner cabinet in the dining area. Of course, the crystal glassware was always visible through the glass panes of the upper cupboard doors.* Remembering the built-in version at Principio as I reached for the knob on the bottom door, I knew I would find the china there, in stacks.

I dashed back to my seat, anticipating the scrape of Ag's walker in the foyer, but instead Allie reappeared to say that Ag had returned to bed. Normally she would come out to greet me. My brain debated whether to go back and see her. Was she simply tired? Was she hoping I'd come back alone? Or was she so confused that she'd already forgotten I was there? In the end I chose to let a sleeping cancer patient lie. I wrote in my journal:

I imagine that mental breakdown is necessary for Ag to physically let go of her body and her life in this realm. Her impulse to control is just too strong otherwise. A sudden wave of regret grips me with the realization that the opportunity for a final, solo conversation might well be past, and I missed it. The welling up of sobs takes me by surprise. Why exactly am I crying? What are these tears saying to me? Suddenly, I understand that Ag's passing will be a big moment in my life. I can never unknow her or undo her impact. A new question arises from a place of great wisdom and gentleness: What do I need to do for myself to mark this significant passage?

The caregiver, Tessa, answered the phone when I called on a Saturday morning in early June. "Hi, I'm just checking in. My siblings and I want to drop by as a group in a little while. My older brother and his wife are in town. How's Ag this morning? Could she cope with this?"

Audrey had strongly urged this overture when she got wind of Mike and Sharon's visit, and with the safety of numbers I was willing to proceed.

"That should be fine," Tessa said. "She's up, and we're fixing breakfast."

An hour later when we arrived, however, they were in the bedroom, and breakfast had not been eaten. Ag looked disheveled, wearing the same pajamas as the Saturday back in January when she had entered the hospital with fever and delirium. As we trooped in one after another, she looked up, openmouthed, and then her face crumpled into tears.

"Am I dying?" she asked, sounding anguished. I hung back while Mike and then Tessa said things like, "You're okay, everything's fine."

Casting about from one face to another, she asked again, with greater urgency, "Am I dying?"

She needs the truth, I thought, and I moved to sit beside her on the bed and rubbed her arm gently. "Your disease is progressing. Yes, you're in the process now," I said.

Her speech was labored and only partially intelligible as she pressed on with questions. Finally, I understood one of them, asked in a hopeful-sounding tone, "Did someone tell you to come here?" She was wondering if hospice had called us because her death was imminent.

"No," I said, taken aback, "Mike and Sharon are in town, so we all just came together."

Standing up from the bed, I explained her query to the group. As if scripted, one by one, everyone was beckoned to her side for a personal conversation. I was in and out of the room and wasn't sure I'd have a turn since I'd already occupied the spot next to her. But yes, she called for me, and I leaned over, again rubbing her arm that was mostly bone, her shoulder and clavicle prominent too, not sure what would transpire. Was this really happening?

The first thing she uttered was clear enough, though jarring: "I want to love you."

Uncertain of her meaning, I accepted it neutrally. She struggled to say more, but I comprehended only a fragment, "like a mother." Rather than seek clarification, I said only, "It's all okay. You just rest now." Before ceding the spot next to her on the bed, I hugged her with an air kiss and reflexively said, "I love you."

I puzzled over her words for days, in my journal and out loud with Joe. I could not make any sense of them. Ag and I did not speak again as she entered a final descent that progressed more like a river than a roller coaster, its movement swift but smooth, gentler than *whooshing*. We transferred her to the hospice inpatient facility three days later, a decision in which she was unable to participate. In the middle of this move, a long-ago memory from Michael's preschool days in Yvonne's room surfaced, and I kept hearing four-year-old Michael's singsong voice at the end of the school year, reporting in a pleased, almost satisfied tone of voice, "We hugged the kindargarters g'bye." As Ag entered her last days, I heard it as "We took an action to mark a transition."

At the hospice facility, a setting devoid of personal history, a ritual gesture felt possible in a way it had not at the condo, and I knew what I wanted to do. A Healing Touch technique called the Chakra Spread releases energy to aid transitions and is specifically appropriate for the dying. Ag had been intermittently agitated during transport to hospice but then settled into deep sleep, and I realized it was now or never.

The Chakra Spread is done while standing next to the person and then, over various points along their body, bringing your palms down slowly toward them but without touching and then pushing your hands apart away from each other: Over the crown of the head, the brow, the throat, the heart, the solar plexus, the sacrum, the root, and then the knees and ankles. Three times over each, followed by lightly pulling down with both hands from the person's knees to their feet and out, again without touching. It finishes by holding their hand and placing yours on their heart. Ag was snugly covered, so I just placed my hands approximately in these areas. I felt no strong emotion, only wordless calm.

Five days later, hospice staff summoned us to the bedside for continuous vigil due to changes in Ag's breathing. Over the course of that summer solstice evening, we witnessed her respiration gradually slow. Finally, at 11:39 at night, the last puff came, and the sudden absence of the soft sound that for hours had absorbed our attention left a startling void.

"I think she's gone," I said.

This time Mark and I alone headed up the arrangements, using Dad's as a template. The visitation was well attended by our friends, Ag's friends, and relatives of all branches of our family, including everyone's in-laws and various colleagues and contacts. The funeral mass unfolded smoothly. None of us chose to speak. I was too worn out and my feelings were too conflicted to compose a coherent message. The current pastor had known Ag and provided a personal touch in his homily. Two previous pastors for whom Ag had worked during her eleven years as parish secretary joined him at the altar. Then on to the cemetery for a brief service before gathering at our house.

The Art of Reassembly

In midafternoon, Joe and I and our kids plopped on our living room furniture after I closed the door on the last guests departing the post-funeral lunch. "Is anyone still here? Are all the guests gone?" I said loudly as I turned the lock, echoing our custom from years earlier when we hosted group activities with moms and kids. Whenever guests left en masse, a distinct type of silence descended, and that peace now enveloped us. I looked around at the faces of my beloved children and spouse, claiming this interlude as a precious gift.

To my astonishment, the usual post-event chatting went far beyond comments about food or tidbits of conversation. My grown children said how amazing I had been and how they were glad for me that this challenging chapter had ended. Their words were so unexpected that I could not absorb them specifically, but I comprehended the message: Despite my emotional reactivity and hypervigilance throughout their lives, as young adults now, they got what I had been going through, not only the past few years, but the entire time since my mom died when I was seven years old. I will always remember how seen and understood I felt in this moment.

Too soon, we dispersed. That evening, Michael would drive back to Chicago, his move-in with his girlfriend imminent, though Kieran and Christian were home from college for the summer.

Rising from the couch, Kieran said firmly, "Can we put out a picture of Mary Lee now? I think we should put your parents' wedding picture in the front hall."

Chapter Twenty-Three

Following the funeral, I gave myself a week to recover before returning to the condo. Other building residents had already queried about our plans for the unit, and I had told several people, "We'll be selling it, but realistically not until fall." In the middle of a scorching late-June afternoon, I drove over alone, declining Joe's offer to accompany me. Parking as usual and using my keys to enter, I had the sense of a furtive act for reasons I could not name. I encountered no neighbors and slipped silently into the condo's air-conditioned coolness, where unforeseen serenity greeted me. When Ag moved to the inpatient hospice, Audrey had removed the medicine dispenser that had stood on the hutch for months like a mantel clock marking the hours. Allie had orchestrated pickup of other equipment, and the queen bed was not only restored to its normal position but also made up with the blue-and-white-striped comforter and matching pillows that had been stowed away for nearly a year. I had forgotten that Ag's cleaner had come a few days earlier as well. The floors gleamed, and a lemon fragrance lingered in the air. Time telescoped as a fleeting sense of Dad and Ag, in robust health and relishing their river view, hovered just beyond my awareness.

The Art of Reassembly

This was a reconnaissance mission. I wandered slowly through each room, opened cupboards and drawers, just looking. In the study, I noted that boxes on the closet floor had long ago replaced the old file cabinet for photo storage. I lingered over the shelf of photo albums and the built-in cabinets below, in which I discovered a cache of memorabilia. Amid stacks of Ag's personal albums and folders, a few more treasures of Mary Lee surfaced. I inhaled quickly, realizing I held a program from her high school graduation, her diploma, and my parents' 1955 wedding album. In the same moment, I knew these items needed to be shared with everyone. I could not snatch them up for myself as I had the wedding book. Carefully, I restacked everything and closed the cabinet door, my body humming with anticipation. What other portals to the past would I find?

A plan began to formulate itself, a logical order of tasks to empty this place and distribute its contents to my siblings and me equitably, remove whatever remained, and market the condo. The previous fall, I had watched Joe oversee a similar process as executor of his aunt's estate, and it had worked well. My parents' 1500-square-foot unit was not stuffed, but I had moved enough times to recognize it would take time to process everything. Thoughts organized, I returned home.

If only the emotional aspects were as straightforward. "I'm not grieving for Ag," I had told myself resolutely after the funeral. Caregiving had ended; I was free. Wiser instinct understood that adrenaline covered more complex feelings, and I could not help but notice my erratic emotions. Why in the world did I fume so about the lackadaisical lifeguards at our swim club? Why was I so impatient with the airline employees on the phone? And short with Joe over nothing? Finally, over the July Fourth weekend, I lounged in the recliner all morning on Saturday, reading an actual library book and drinking coffee, and then went swimming for the afternoon. It was like a big exhale after months of holding tight.

Now, a week later, I was back at the condo preparing to accompany Mark and Laura through, totally aware of mounting agitation. After more than four decades, Dad's first and second marriages would collide in the posthumous distribution of possessions. I had already toured with my other siblings, and a legal pad listed their requested items. After today I would compile them into a single spreadsheet. Upon arrival, I raised the blinds on the condo's eye-catching view and switched lamps on in the rear rooms, which were in shade. The condo still smelled fresh from its cleaning, no longer weighed down by illness. I returned to the front room to wait and gazed out at the sparkling water from a bucket-style chair in the sitting area, remembering how much Dad, gone three years now, loved to watch barges going by in both directions. I realized yet again that my current seat and its mate, plus the love seat, had been purchased by my mom for the house we lived in on Raeburn Drive. The provenance of everything in this condo plagued me. The dining table also dated from Raeburn.

When Mark and Laura came in, their taut faces conveyed unease. I was mindful of Mark's devotion to Ag and how hard this first time here since her death must be. As I had done, they walked slowly, meditatively through the rooms, and Laura remarked, "Why does it feel better here? Is it just because it's clean and the lights are on?"

"I don't know exactly, but I feel it too." I replied.

I picked up the legal pad, ready to accomplish our purpose, and Mark spoke his fear of relationships being divided along with property. "I know nothing. I do not know anything about where anything came from. I need you to tell me."

"I'm confident we can divide everything amicably," I said, outwardly reassuring though still stirred up inside. As we perused the condo, I heard myself using strange euphemisms about the origins of various items—"before," "Raeburn," or "the first marriage"— that caused them to shrug and move on. I heard myself promoting "Ag and Al" items, my unspoken code for "things they received for their wedding" or "things they acquired together." I never actually stated, "That belonged to my real mother, and I don't want you to have it." Did I really mean that anyway? I had no idea.

Eventually I was able to state clearly to them as I had to everyone else, "If you have the slightest interest in something, then write it down. No one is going to get everything they want, but the goal is to give people the things that mean the most to them."

In the dining area, we came to a set of four framed still-life fruit prints on the side wall, two flanking each side of the window—apple, pear, grapes, and peach.

"What's the history of these?" Laura asked, her voice tentative.

"They were at Raeburn," I replied truthfully.

"Oh, okay," she said, meeting Mark's eyes and shaking her head ever so slightly.

"If you like these, you should request them," I heard myself say. With visions of their downstairs in my mind, I added, "They are your taste."

"If we received them, they would hang in our home," Laura acknowledged.

"Just because something is from Raeburn doesn't mean you can't have it," I said, meaning it. "I'm writing these down: Four fruit prints from dining room."

That first round with my siblings, dealing with mostly practical items like furniture and housewares, was just the top layer in a process that unfolded in phases resembling an archeological dig. With those initial selections complete, the next steps in clearing the condo moved down into lower strata. Many pieces of furniture stayed in place for eventual real estate showings, and we deferred highly sentimental items like photos until later. Ag's neighbors continued to express curiosity about when we would sell, but I still held them off. I had to pace myself, as I could only do so much at once before exhaustion set in.

I went over alone to pack up Ag's clothing, determined to cross a significant category off the list. Working drawer by drawer and then on to the closet, in assembly-line fashion, I tossed sweaters, slacks, blouses, and shoes into large green trash bags. Faded T-shirts, pajamas, bras, and underwear I simply pitched. *Just keep going*, I said silently. Perhaps the vulnerability of this task was the reason I preferred doing it by myself. I left the pile of shoeboxes on the bedroom floor to be dealt with another time, then lugged the green bags to the car, dropping them at Goodwill on the way home.

I accepted Tim's offer of help to empty the kitchen and came prepared with moving boxes and packing materials from Home Depot. We stood in the middle of the room, both of us surveying the cabinets, considering.

Tim began with the ones above the sink that held dishes. "Oh gosh, look at this!" he said, holding up a single salad-size white plate painted with a thick brown stripe around the edge. "The 'wooden' plate!"

As kids, we had taken turns eating frozen waffles and peanut butter and jelly sandwiches off that coveted dish. I looked up from the drawer of utensils I had been digging through and smiled. "Go ahead and take that if you want," I said.

"Good lord!" I exclaimed soon after, lifting first a soup ladle with a faux wood handle, a once-white but now-quite-yellowed plastic serving spoon, and an aluminum cheese slicer. All of these dated back more than forty years to Raeburn Drive before Dad's remarriage. I felt the heft of the cheese slicer, still in pristine shape, noted its wire that I had pressed through blocks of Velveeta for grilled cheese sandwiches. Soon we each had a little pile in the living room. The soup ladle went to charity and the plastic spoon to the trash, but I took the cheese slicer, and Tim the wooden plate.

The aura of these artifacts created a kind of dream state in which sepia-toned memories shimmered. Scenes of Tim and me in the back seat of our mom's dark green 1966 Mustang driving to the grocery store while Mike and Kate were at school. The two of us coloring or playing with Play-Doh in the utility room while Mom cooked dinner. Tim taking naps while I stayed up in the afternoons; Mom watching soap operas and smoking cigarettes. She had an ashtray that was brown glass surrounded by textured green cloth. The bottom was squishy like a beanbag, not firm and molded. Sometimes she ironed as she watched the soaps. She ironed the sheets and also Dad's shirts, his handkerchiefs, and even his boxer shorts and T-shirts. She and I did not talk much during these interludes. I curled up with a blanket on the couch resting without falling asleep, probably sucking my thumb.

Tim moved on to the high cabinets over the refrigerator and pulled out a seemingly endless collection of tan Pfaltzgraff dishes and accessories.

"What on earth is all this? Why did she have so much of it?"

"She bought those dishes starting around the late 1970s. I'm not really sure why. Don't you remember? We used them for holidays with that hideous brown tablecloth."

We returned to our work, quiet for a bit, until I ventured a more delicate inquiry. "Do you ever think about the adoption?"

"All the time," he said without hesitation. "I wish so much I could go back and say no, I don't want my birth certificate changed."

"Yeah, that's exactly how I feel," I said.

Brushing away tears, he continued, "I feel bad and guilty, like I turned my back on our mom, but in reality, I couldn't have said no. The only possible answer was yes."

Nodding agreement, and comforted by his unequivocal response, I replied, "The older I get, the more it bothers me about the birth certificate. I've tried to research whether adoption can be undone, but I don't think it can."

"Really?" He looked up from wrapping plates, eyebrows raised. "Let me know if you ever find out anything more."

Chapter Twenty-Four

Iknelt on the textured cream carpet before the buffet as if it were a vault. It had been another afternoon of digging at the condo. I pressed the corners of the compartments at either end, heard the familiar *click*, and leaned back, smiling, as they swung out automatically. Inside, the treasures sat waiting for rediscovery. I pulled out silver trays, goblets, candlesticks, and other serving items, removed the plastic coverings to reveal their gleaming finish, then arranged them for photographing, singly and in groupings of similar objects. I would create a catalogue of pictures and brief descriptions of these fine items for my siblings and myself to use in making selections.

Moving on to the dark-stained hutch in the corner, I opened the lower doors to reveal my mother's creamy gold-rimmed Lenox china with the pink rose in the center. The felt circles that had always fascinated me continued to cushion the stacked plates, transporting me back to the dining room at Raeburn. I snapped out of this reverie and resumed my task, photographing the set, then shut the doors and stood to open the top, where the delicate crystal wine glasses and water goblets were stored. Lastly, I retrieved the cordovan-stained wood chest of sterling flatware from the foyer closet. I held one of the forks in my palm for a moment, then finished taking photos.

In short order, I cut and pasted the pictures into a Word document with a few lines of text for each but wrestled with my personal selections over the ensuing weeks. The long-awaited claiming of maternal heirlooms now seemed anticlimactic as the thrill of discovery hardened to resentment. *These things sat for years without being used! I've always wanted the china and silver, but now I'm not sure. I want them to make me closer to my mom, but they don't. I want them to erase the pain of loss, but they won't. Ag is dead but never gone. My heritage was altered forever.* These mental gyrations also created further uncertainty about the furniture selections I had made previously. *Do we really need a different dining room set? Even though the two bucket chairs are from Raeburn, would I accomplish anything by bringing them to our house now?* The corner cabinet was a definite though, at Kieran's insistence.

"Mom, please choose it. I'd really like to have it someday," she'd said early on and continued to remind me.

At home, hosting friends for dinner precipitated a much-needed tidying up. Mail had piled up significantly at the end of the kitchen peninsula, and there were stacks on the table in the family room, remnants from more than a month earlier. Rather than restack and shove it farther away, I took time to go through all the mail, particularly the various statements from financial institutions. Reviewing the statements, I became confused about a couple things and fixated particularly on information that seemed inconsistent. In a fit of pique, I dashed off an email to our advisors demanding to know why. Joe was at his desk next to mine, and I kept up a verbal rant as I crafted sentences on the screen. Editing here and there, I started to see myself with curiosity, as if a separate self were checking in, very gently. *What is going on? A tirade like this often has an underlying cause, a hurt that needs expression.* I stopped typing and turned to look at Joe, my eyes brimming with tears.

"I think . . . this is really about something else," I said haltingly, my breath caught with swallowed sobs. "I'm just really upset about my parents' stuff, the china and the silver. . . . Every time I think about it . . . I feel angry." I broke down, doubled over in my desk chair with wrenching tears.

Then the wise voice inside whispered a reminder that anger is part of grief, and the underlying truth ripped through me. Stricken, I said, "Oh, my god, this feels like losing my mom again, as though it's just happened."

Always before I had cried for my past self, for the lost, motherless girl, but sitting there at that minute, I wept as though for a present loss, until anger yielded to irresolvable heartache. I thought of someone I knew whose preemie twins died shortly after birth, my classmate who recently lost her husband. "This is just how it feels, the reality of grief, the finality of death," I said to myself, oddly comforted by feeling "normal" in my emotions. Joe came over and hugged me. Starting to calm, taking deep breaths, I wiped my eyes, then clicked the trash-can icon on the draft email, shut the laptop, and stood up from the desk. I didn't have to make final choices about heirlooms or furniture right away; there was still time to consider.

Just after Labor Day, I shared with the other building residents that we were ready for referrals. In my own home, I stared at the walls and wandered the rooms considering my choices. *What would be meaningful? What is there space for?* Our existing dining room set fit our style and included two buffets that were integral to serving holiday meals and storing dishes and trays. I measured the heirloom table and plotted its placement. *Too wide*, I concluded. *No, I don't want it.* Only one possible corner was available for the cabinet, and it would fit perfectly.

On move-out day at the condo, right after Thanksgiving, I sat for the last time in one of the bucket chairs, looking at the river. We had accepted an offer from friends of the couple next door, so the condo never even went on the market. My siblings and I removed our remaining items, and I hired the crew now making quick work of the back rooms. The sun was coming up in the east, behind me, and ahead on the horizon, the downtown skyscrapers looked like a magical city off in the distance. My position in this chair evoked memories of Dad, legs crossed, steepled fingers at his chin, taking in the view he loved so much. These chairs would not reside in my home. Whatever configuration I imagined, they never seemed to quite belong, like pieces of a jigsaw that could not find the right niche. I started to feel weepy, but then calm certainty rose with the sun. It was time to step forward from this place.

The truck delivered items first to Goodwill, then to a charity consignment store, to my sister's apartment, and finally to our house, filling the dining room with boxes containing my selections, still-to-be-sorted photos and memorabilia, and miscellaneous remnants. I had taken possession of the china, sterling flatware, and crystal, at least for now. None of my siblings had asked for them, and I could always move any or all of it along later if I chose.

The upcoming Christmas holiday gave me no choice but to dive in and figure out where to put everything. After Joe helped me push the corner cabinet into place, being able to walk around the room again seemed a hopeful sign, so I began yanking packing tape off the cartons. Then everything slowed as the process captivated me. I fetched cotton cloths and supplies to wipe the shelves inside the cabinet and dust the exterior till it shone. *Thank goodness Kieran pushed for the corner cabinet*, I soon realized, restoring the stacks of pink-rose plates and bowls to the lower compartment. I didn't know where else I could have stored them. I smiled at the thought of passing these heirlooms to my daughter, suddenly knowing that I would do it during my lifetime, when she was settled in a home and perhaps ready to host holidays herself.

Next, I unzipped the quilted cases holding the crystal water goblets and started to place them one by one on the glass shelf in the upper section, but then my fingers sensed stickiness. Closer examination revealed murky dust, so I took them to the kitchen to wash. Soaping the green scrubby pad and wetting it generously, I dampened the first glass and then rubbed it gently all around the inner and outer surfaces and stem, rinsed it in warm water, and set it upside down on a towel I had laid flat.

Unhurried, I handled each one individually. The water goblets dried quickly, so I turned them upright, struck by their sparkly sheen. I moved on to the wine glasses, and a loosening in my body accompanied the grime's dissolution as I applied the soapy scrub pad, then rinsed. I held a wine glass up to the light, finally filled with delight to possess all these beautiful items. Of course, I wanted them. How could I have considered otherwise? Their clarity became a window, drawing me more deeply into the past.

PART FOUR

Chapter Twenty-Five

When I met my mom's two younger sisters for lunch at the bookstore café, I carried a canvas tote bag containing treasures of Mary Lee I had unearthed in the condo. Eventually these items would be divided with my siblings. We hadn't had time yet to properly go over them together, so for now I could pursue my personal curiosity with Judy and Jeanne, who were seven and nine years younger than my mom, both in their seventies now. First, we opened my parents' album of black-and-white wedding photos, all eight-by-tens, one per page. As the two of them sat side by side gazing at each image, small smiles on their faces, I caught glimpses of the "little girls" they had been in relation to my mom.

"Remember, Mom's dress was dark green," Judy said, pointing to my grandma in a picture.

"And the bridesmaid dresses were a gold color," Jeanne added.

They chuckled and shook their heads over how young everyone looked. My mom's twin brother, Bill, was in France at the time, serving in the army. As a surprise, he called on the phone that morning and talked to Mary, which was a big deal, they said. It had to be arranged in advance. I hadn't noted his absence in the pictures, but sure enough that was the case.

"It was hard on him not to be there, but Mary and Al had already waited two years while your dad was in the army," Judy said.

We set the memorabilia aside to eat our quiche and chat about other topics, and I willed myself to release the old strangeness that licked at me like waves on the shore. I was no longer a confused twelve-year-old. I had initiated this get-together. As a grown-up, I sensed their genuine pleasure at being with me. When the plates were cleared, we wiped the water rings from the table and moved the glasses, and I brought out the rest. They spent considerable time perusing the wedding-gifts book, recollecting relatives and neighbors and specific gifts that had impressed them, like the silver. Now we had traveled to the edge of safety. I had come without conscious agenda other than sharing these vintage articles, but the moment suddenly felt ripe for a deeper dive.

"I'm sorry to introduce a sad note, but I'm wondering, what was it like when she got sick? What do you remember from that time?"

Jeanne responded most, because Judy had been a religious sister then, more removed from the situation.

"Well, she was diagnosed in the summer of 1968. She and your dad came home from a business trip early so she could have surgery. Mary had found a lump. Then the doctor found a second one when he examined her. During surgery they found a third, and this one that they hadn't seen was the malignancy. She woke up bound like a mummy. The initial results were positive, it was benign, but they wanted to remove her ovaries, too, so she had that done right away while she was already there."

"That fits with a fuzzy memory I have of my fifth birthday. We had a party at home. You and Grandma and Grandpa came over, and there was a bakery cake with white frosting and pink roses, which I loved. But my mom was in her robe and had been in the hospital," I said, and Jeanne nodded.

Mentally, I connected dots but did not share aloud: I had entered kindergarten within weeks of turning five. Considering that event from my mom's perspective now, in the context of her cancer diagnosis, her doting impulse to come pick me up and then her allowing of my independence touched me deeply.

Even with their age difference, my mom and Jeanne had shared a room growing up because, according to Judy, "I was a brat and had to have my own room." In high school, when my mom invited a friend for an overnight, the other girl slept in my mom's bed and my mom would climb in with Jeanne. The two teens would talk, and Jeanne overheard all kinds of things about boyfriends and so forth. Once, feeling daring, she remarked in public, "I hear a lot of things." In a tone both flattering and warning, Mary had replied, "And you would never tell anyone what you hear."

Jeanne shared this story to illustrate the long history of trust between the two of them. In what became the final months of my mom's illness, after she began having violent headaches and then the seizure that caused her collapse in the kitchen, she asked Jeanne to find a medical textbook left from her nursing studies, rather than worrying my dad with the request.

"She read through it, then closed the book and said, 'Now I know for sure. The cancer is in my brain.' No one had told her this," Jeanne said.

Later my mom phoned a doctor friend who was not one of her caregivers to talk it over. When he called back, he got Dad, who was confused about why he was calling, but the doctor went on to say firmly that the cancer had metastasized to her brain, which was the first my dad had heard of it.

Now perched ramrod straight on the edge of my seat, legs crossed, and hands folded in front of me on the table, I had no idea what time it was or how long Judy and Jeanne were available to stay and talk, but there was no turning back now.

"What did you think when Dad remarried? Did you think that was a good thing?"

They both just stared at me, but I plowed on.

"I'm at a point in my life where I need to tell the truth about what happened to me. I need to say that it was hard. Some parts were okay or even good, but Ag was not always nice. I just need to tell at least some people honestly that it was hard."

My voice caught, and a few tears gathered in the corners of my eyes. They looked at me wordlessly, so I kept talking.

"I can empathize with people who were there—for my dad, for you all, who lived through it. But I cannot excuse Ag in the same way. She had not experienced the terrible loss. By the time they married, I had become this overly mature, responsible child. It made me feel better to exert control over my environment, to fix dinner the way I thought it should be done if Mike wasn't home, or to make sure Tim did his homework. I wasn't Cinderella being forced to do all those things, though Dad probably liked that I did. But Ag made use of me for her own convenience."

They continued to sit like statues. Still, I went on speaking.

"I became disconnected from the Wimberg cousins. We never had holidays again with all of you. The times I saw my cousins after we were all grown, I realized all the history that had continued without me. I felt like I didn't belong. Ag's family was genuinely nice to me. Her sisters treated me like their own niece. But when I got older and more disconnected from Ag, I clearly saw that they were not my family. And I'd lost Grandma too. I would go visit her and she would sit silently at the table. It was awful. So I stopped going."

Jeanne's eyebrows knitted together. "I remember Mom calling me once after you moved, very happy, saying, 'Guess who came by today for lunch?'"

"It was fine at first, but then later it became very uncomfortable,"

I said. "Much later I thought that the change for her after Dad was married, not being involved in our day-to-day lives anymore, made her confront her own grief about the death of her daughter, and she became depressed."

Jeanne flinched, her tone suddenly sharp. "*No, that's not* how it was!"

I recoiled slightly and started to pull back from the obviously sensitive subject. Instead, I allowed her terse words to hang over the table. Then I persisted gently, "Please, tell me what happened. Tell me the truth."

"We were shut out," she finally spat.

I did not tremble or tingle or freeze up.

"That makes sense," I said, releasing an audible exhale and leaning back in my chair.

Jeanne said, her calm demeanor returning, "To answer your original question: In my head, I wanted to be happy and think the marriage was a good thing, but Mom and I cried and cried that night after your dad came and told her."

Departing, we exchanged extended hugs, and I said several times, "Thank you so much. I feel relieved to know the truth, finally."

At home that evening I regaled Joe with the tale. "You are never going to *believe* what I heard today!" However, unfolding the revelation to him, it seemed less a triumphant victory and more of a blow. Over the ensuing weeks, my heart ached. I needed help. On impulse, through online searching I found that Donna Jackson, my former therapist from years earlier, still practiced in the same converted house not far away. "I was your client twenty-five years ago after I first began dealing with my mom's death when I was a child. I need to revisit some of the things we discussed then," I wrote to her in an email.

The office had been redecorated of course, and Dr. Jackson

could not locate my previous file after so long an interval. In fact, I don't think she remembered me at all, but I didn't care. Her steady, steely poise remained reliably the same. Seated once more on the couch across from her, my story now opened to painful reinterpretation, I stood in a vast field of rubble, slowly picking up one piece after another to examine each one anew. How could I fashion them into a coherent whole?

The first Thanksgiving and Christmas, with my dad's blessing, Ag introduced new patterns of celebration that pushed my mom's family to the periphery, permanently. At our recent lunch, Jeanne recalled that initially Ag had said all the right things when Grandma expressed her desire to still see us, had assured her she would always be our grandmother, so they were taken aback that first round of holidays.

"We didn't know if it was coming from your dad or what, possibly wanting to let her do her own thing that first year. But then that was it," Jeanne had said.

Going forward, we had a gift-exchange event with my grandparents, in the afternoon of Christmas Eve or Christmas Day, a separate, unequal way of staying connected. We never again gathered with our Wimberg aunts, uncles, and cousins as part of the main holiday, and my mom's parents were never invited to our birthdays. The adoption had been so tenderly presented as for my welfare should anything happen to Dad. How much of that was sincere? Was it also a tactic to exclude the Wimbergs from our future? At lunch, when I mentioned my adult regrets about the adoption to Judy and Jeanne, their mouths had gaped as they stared at me wide-eyed. They had had no idea of the impact on my birth certificate.

To Dr. Jackson, I said, "The adoption hid my mom; not just the paperwork, but the whole mindset behind it harmed me more than the fact of her death. My dad and Ag harmed me."

She tilted her head. "Do you think it was on purpose to hurt you? Of course, you were hurt, but was that the intent, do you think?"

"I . . . don't know," I said, caught off guard by the question and stiffening in resistance to seeing a different perspective.

She didn't pursue that angle further. Instead, she said, "Do you want to talk to Ag? We could do that."

At my confused expression, she gestured to the empty chair next to her and said, "We could pretend she's sitting right there, and you could tell her what you need to say."

Shuddering with a visceral, reflexive fear, I paused before replying, "Maybe. Not today."

"Okay," Dr. Jackson said, nodding.

Not only during therapy appointments, but also while lying in bed at night or in the predawn hours, I wrestled with questions about Ag and Dad's actions over and over. Speculatively, I conjured the early days still at Raeburn. Did Ag and Dad consciously plan the distancing? Did they discuss it behind closed doors in their bedroom or in the family room during the eleven o'clock news, or even at Ag's apartment before the wedding? Or did it come about indirectly, understood through what was not said rather than words expressly stated? During their courtship, Dad might have groused from time to time about his in-laws, even mildly, and perhaps she sensed a desire for independence that meshed with her own preferences. Maybe he didn't complain, but she picked up on how integral they were to his children's lives and felt threatened. Possibly the fact of being someone's second wife caused festering insecurity. Or some combination of all these scenarios.

After they married, of course he wanted Ag to be content, grateful to have her as a companion and helpmate with his four children. He wanted the happy ending. I imagined them downstairs in the basement at Principio, seated at either ends of the couch with glasses of wine, she in her bathrobe working the crossword, chatting about whom to invite for an upcoming holiday or birthday, Dad nodding agreeably. On another night, maybe Dad reported on a phone call with the lawyer, elaborating the benefits of adopting us and outlining the necessary steps, Ag nodding this time, then clarifying with questions, jotting notes. Had Dad ever noticed the fluffy white guest towels with Mary Lee's monogram turning into gray rags from everyday use?

At home, Joe listened patiently to my recurring analysis that inevitably dead-ended at the bewildering question: What to do with the knowledge that my father and stepmother cut me off from my maternal lineage? Finally, there among the ruins of my story, I knew I had to keep digging.

Chapter Twenty-Six

Once again, I drove west from my home to revisit significant childhood locations. Though this time I did not stop at the library where I had first obtained a library card with my mom, a rush of gratitude filled me as I passed it. My lifelong love of books and libraries had started in that building, with her, I realized, amazed. From there, I could trace my life path in books, beginning with the literature that created refuge from sadness as a child, to the various works on birthing, parenting, mother loss, and grief that helped me unfold my emotions in adulthood. It was a rich legacy from my mom that I had not considered before.

Continuing a few miles farther, I arrived at Little Flower Parish, noticing once more how my palms tingled and my heart rate accelerated. I understood the anxiety better this time. I had enrolled in this school with a mother like everyone else, and I experienced her loss here. My classmates attended her funeral. When I returned to school a few days later, everyone fussed over me, which I both loved and loathed, because deep down I knew that I had become irrevocably different from everyone else. My grandma's name was added to the Girl Scout troop contact list in the mother column with a big asterisk and "grandmother" in

181

parentheses, so my name took up extra space in the chart. Mrs. Newman picked us up every day. All my responsibility and care-taking, desperate attempts to make everyone okay, especially myself, were connected to this place. When Dad remarried and we moved across town, we boxed up the sorrow. We left behind the outward "difference" and became a nuclear family that looked more like everyone else, though the pain and grief remained, just more deeply buried.

Recently I had discovered that the parish website included staff emails. Repeatedly I had hovered the mouse over the parish secretary's address, hesitant. Finally, I went for it and emailed to request a visit to the former school building, acknowledging that it was probably an unusual one. "My mom died of breast cancer when I was in second grade there, and I find myself exploring this childhood loss yet again."

We had easily arranged this appointment. The secretary's name was Beth. Following her instructions to the letter, I appeared at the door on time. The rectory, unfamiliar territory to me, was but a brief stop. Beth pulled a large key ring out of her top desk drawer, grabbed her jacket from a hook on the wall, and led me out, down the stairs, and across the drive between church and school.

"I really appreciate your time to do this," I said, trying to sound businesslike, as though I were a journalist on assignment, to alleviate self-consciousness and mask vulnerability.

"I don't mind," Beth replied, friendly, as though she regularly toured former students from four decades ago. "It's good for me to get over here once in a while to check on things, make sure there's no burst pipes or anything."

We descended a flight of concrete stairs leading into the cafeteria. Beth was uncertain about the lights, and the shadowy dark and chill of the sprawling space unsettled me at first. I stood still, letting my eyes adjust. I took in the dingy, scuffed walls in desperate need of paint and the brown speckled linoleum floor that I remembered, the empty trophy cases across the room. Then Beth's voice cut in, sounding almost impatient, "So, what was it you wanted to see?"

I so wished to be alone! It felt impossible to say, *I just want to commune with the space, to see what comes up for me.* Instead, I settled for, "Nothing in particular. I'd just like to walk through."

"Well, since you were only here to sixth grade, you weren't in the junior high wing," she said, gesturing across to a door, "and I'm not sure I have the key for that anyway."

Comprehending that her generosity had limits, I did not contradict her with the fact that my sixth-grade classroom had been in the newer wing. That part of the building did not interest me all that much. She led the way to a short set of stairs to the right, which is the route I would have chosen, too. We passed the door I had normally entered on school mornings and continued up to the classrooms of the older part of the building. The floors were carpeted up there, which was different than I remembered. Looking through the windows of the locked classroom doors, I saw brightly colored walls that contrasted with the dull cream of my youth. But the dark woodwork of the shelves beneath the windows and the coat closets along one wall began to spiral me back.

Pointing to the end of the hall, Beth said, "The statue of St. Therese is still there at the end of the hall. I don't know if you remember that. We had another school that rented this part of the building for a couple years, and we required that it stay."

"Yes, I do," I said, continuing to peek into the classrooms where I was a third and fifth grader, not sure which was which, but sinking deeper into something. Slowing my steps and avoiding her gaze, I walked toward the statue, clearly recalling that to the right a few steps down led to the classroom area where I had been in second grade and fourth grade. Beth followed me there.

"I'd really like to see these rooms. Would you mind unlocking this door?" I spoke decisively, issuing a directive rather than a request.

She obliged without comment. The space seemed so much smaller than I remembered. The room in the back had been my second-grade classroom, and I walked through as if led by an invisible thread. In the corner to the left, the little raised area where we had had reading in small groups suddenly seemed so familiar that I almost gasped aloud. The sense of presence grew stronger as we left those rooms and descended a different set of stairs that exited by the bathrooms. A quick left and we were on the ramp leading back into the cafeteria. As I braced my adult legs on the downward slope, body memory took over. I was seven years old, lined up with my class along the right wall for lunch, the smell of meatloaf and mashed potatoes or hot dogs and french fries hanging in the air. Whether we bought the full plate or just milk, everyone filed through from the entry door on the right at the bottom of the ramp. I could only view the kitchen through the window, marveling mentally at how small it seemed.

Back in the cafeteria, I pondered the alcove where I attended Girl Scout meetings after school in fourth, fifth, and sixth grades, but Beth's voice slashed through my reverie.

"You can just leave through the same door we came in. I need to make sure all the doors are locked upstairs," she said.

"Oh, okay. Thanks so much again," I said, taking the not-so-subtle hint that the visit had ended.

"You're welcome. I hope you got what you wanted out of it," she replied, sounding doubtful.

"Bye."

I returned to my car feeling strange, almost feverish, then drove a short distance and parked on a side street. I wanted to absorb the experience while it was still fresh. For a moment, I wished I had taken pictures. Recalling the previous parking lot photos, I quickly realized that a camera could not have captured anything worthwhile. On impulse I had brought my journal, so I jotted down words and phrases attempting to describe what I had seen and felt, including rough sketches of the floor plans. Something quickened. In the dreary halls and abandoned classrooms, my seven-year-old-self had shimmered. Yes, I had seen her, and I understood that she needed me to keep searching.

Since I was in the area, I drove to Mt. Airy public school just around the corner and up the road a short distance, only to find that it had been torn down and completely rebuilt during a massive facilities project undertaken by the school district in recent years. Chagrined by this discovery, I was unable to revisit the playground site of my kindergarten drop-off, though the memory's warmth did not dim.

Chapter Twenty-Seven

My parents' dear friend Rebecca Bowman still lived in the house of my childhood memories, though her husband, John, now resided in a memory-care facility. Just like on Sunday afternoons in the years between my mom's death and Dad's remarriage, I loved entering through the garage when I arrived. The downstairs had been redecorated probably multiple times in the forty-year span since those visits, but the kitchen table and chairs were the same.

"Of course they are," she said when I commented. "I love this set." Still slender and sturdy in her early eighties, Rebecca looked the same to me, too, as we stood chatting. When she gestured to the cupboard and asked, "Would you like a Coke?" I was nine years old again, arriving with Dad and my siblings to be gathered in their embrace. Dad and John had been college friends, and when the two couples bought their first houses in the same neighborhood, she and my mom formed a bond too.

We moved to the kitchen table after she served my drink. "What was my mom like?" I asked, my eyes focused on pouring Coke from a can into a tall glass with ice.

"She was lots of fun. She was a marvelous cook. She loved

children. She adored Al. She shared a lot with me, but I wouldn't call her gabby," Rebecca said, her brown eyes warm and soft. She sat at the head of the table, and I was at her left.

It was hard for me to imagine my mom talking at all, I acknowledged inwardly. To me she was only silent. "I have this image of her as being more reserved, not someone who talked everything out," I said.

"You could say that, I suppose," Rebecca considered, leaning back in her chair. Then she added firmly, "Well, she wasn't afraid to say what she thought. She was a very good friend, I'll tell you that."

"Did you chat on the phone a lot, get together and visit?" I sat still, legs crossed, my forearms on the table, observing her for clues.

"Oh, yes, we talked on the phone every day, and we'd walk to each other's houses. I remember often pushing the stroller over to your house, and we'd have picnic lunches in the backyard."

Rebecca smiled a little, her gaze just past me, as she recollected her friendship with my mom. She looked down at the floor, and her whole body slumped when I asked about my mom's illness. Her account mirrored my aunt's.

"In the summer of 1968, she found a lump. She had a mastectomy and radiation. She did well for about a year. Then she found another lump in the same breast. Eventually it was in her brain, and she had violent headaches. Finally, they put her in the hospital and gave her radiation to try reducing the pain, but there was nothing they could do to save her life at that point. It was so sad. They would put her on a gurney to go receive radiation, and she was in so much pain just being moved."

My mom reacted to her cancer with disbelief, Rebecca said. "'Why me?' is what she felt. She couldn't believe that God would let this happen to her."

Then my mom became very sad. "She was worried about all of you, but especially about Kate, because your mom was the only one who knew braille."

Rebecca teared up at different moments. At one point she said, "I don't want to make you upset with anything I might say."

My reply was swift and firm. "Honestly, it doesn't upset me at all. It's comforting to hear people who knew my mom talk about her. I'm thankful there are still people around to ask."

She recalled the crowd at my mom's visitation, which I did not attend. The casket was open, and my mom looked very pretty in a blue dress, Rebecca said. She also confirmed my impression that Dad spent a lot of time with her and John after my mom died. Sometimes he would drop in when only Rebecca was home.

"The four of us were such close friends. After your mother's death, the three of us became even closer," she said.

"Was it hard for you when Dad remarried?"

"Oh, no, we were happy."

The new foursome did have a close bond through the years, I could see, different than before but genuine in my perception. Until she became too ill, Ag would stop in to see John at his memory-care facility, and Rebecca visited Ag during her final months.

My glass drained, I stood. "Thank you so much for telling me all this. I really appreciate it."

"Oh, you're so welcome. I'm glad to, sweetheart," Rebecca said. We hugged, and I departed through the garage.

Our conversation had confirmed or elaborated much of what I already knew, and I liked that. I kept turning over in my mind the piece that was new, imagining Rebecca and my mom with several young children having picnics in the backyard. I would have been a baby then, but still the image appeared to me in full color. Perhaps it evoked photos I'd seen, or maybe the envisioned scene connected to my own days as a young mom among sippy cups and the sandbox in our yard. Whatever the reason, it felt like a toehold in my mom's life.

Not far away from the Bowmans, Ann Russell and her husband of sixty-two years, Greg, also still resided in the house where they had raised their family, though I had never been there or met them before. Ann had been a college classmate of my mom's whose name I had come across among some memorabilia. Realizing she was the mother of someone a year behind me in high school, I had sought her out, aided by the school alumnae office and then Ann's daughter. Ann and I arranged to meet on a Friday afternoon. Pulling in the driveway, again I adopted my confident air to tamp down nerves, as though this were a business appointment or interview for an article. Ann answered the door looking fit, trim, and spry, round-faced with wide eyes. Her medium bob hair was wispy and gray with remaining traces of brown.

I followed her back to the kitchen, where she told me about her children and grandchildren while she heated soup for Greg's lunch. Her hands shook with tremors, I noticed, and she spilled a little of the soup as she poured from saucepan to bowl. Greg sat at their kitchen table, which was covered with newspapers, including *The Wall Street Journal* and *The New York Times*, working a crossword. The scene conjured up Grandma and Grandpa Wimberg's apartment during my childhood, and I became wistful in the presence of my mom's classmate. What would my mom be like if she were alive today at age eighty-four? I imagined her much like Ann, or like her own mom, tending to home and husband, her life oriented around several generations of family. A deep, middle-aged longing to know my mom as an elder rose quickly and then passed as I refocused my attention on the visit's purpose.

The two of us adjourned to their family room at the back of the house and sat next to each other on the couch. From the coffee table, she picked up a stuffed eight-by-ten photo book with a faux red leather cover and black paper pages, her college album.

Opening it, she caught me off guard by asking, "Did your mom live in the dorm or commute?"

I wondered why she thought I would know if she did not, and my insides cringed with the inadequacy familiar to motherless daughters.

"I don't really know. If I had to guess, I would say commute," I offered.

"I lived in the dorm. I suspect she commuted because she's not in a lot of my pictures."

My heart sank. This did not sound promising.

Ann continued, "We were in the college's first four-year nursing class. The first year was on the school campus, the middle two years were at Good Samaritan Hospital, and then the final year was back at the college."

This was a new detail. Apparently, dorm residence was required at the hospital.

"We used to have picnics at Burnet Woods," Ann recollected fondly, pointing to a series of shots that included my mom, referencing a park that was still located across from the present-day, much-expanded hospital.

"I picked your mom up at home once in the summer to go meet some friends, and we were in a crash not far from their house. Your mom's leg got cut near the knee. She had to get stitches," Ann recalled.

"I remember that scar!" I crowed, "And that it was from a car accident during college!"

When Ann remarked that my mom had been dating my dad for some time, I began to connect some dots from pictures I had seen of my parents at parties during those years, everyone holding a beer in one hand and a cigarette in the other. Suddenly I realized that my mom's social life had been primarily with my dad, her brother Bill, and their friends from a different local college. Somehow this made me a little sad or let down. My mom seemed a person to whom I could not relate, her life defined by a boyfriend and his friends from a young age. Ann's book had several pages depicting a cross-country car trip that she and several others in the class had undertaken one summer. In that moment, my mom's life seemed to compare unfavorably with Ann's path, as though my mom had settled early whereas Ann had been carefree.

Then my perception shifted again as we turned to a photo of five beaming women, seated in a semicircle and wearing bright-colored dresses, opening gifts. Right away I recognized my mom on the right, Ann in the center. Ann had met Greg during the third year of college, and they married a few months before my parents.

"There were a bunch of us who got married right after graduation, so the class had a joint shower," Ann said.

She had set aside a few items for me to take, including a wallet-size portrait of my mom in her nursing uniform with an astonishing note on the back from my mom to Ann: "Best of luck and happiness to you and Greg. Maybe we can get together sometime. I guess recipes and not nursing will be the topic of discussion then. We shall see what we shall see."

I asked, "What do you think she meant by that? Did my mom work after she was married?"

"I don't know. Did she?" Ann seemed jarred by the question, or possibly by my lack of knowledge. She diverted into a story about her own work as a visiting nurse for a couple years, which stopped completely after her second child's birth. As Ann talked, I relaxed a little, realizing that she simply had no frame of reference for early mother loss and the degree of disconnection that I experienced.

"Did you and my mom keep in touch after graduation and marriage?"

"We lived near each other early on, and we played bridge together," Ann said.

Though no longer living close by when my mom was diagnosed with cancer, Ann remembered speaking to her on the phone around that time. "She said she wasn't telling anyone about it until after their upcoming trip to New York."

My parents traveled to a convention each summer with my dad's work, and this timing lined up with Rebecca's and Jeanne's accounts.

"She couldn't believe God would let this happen to her when she already had a blind child," Ann said carefully, watching my face.

"Yes, I've heard that before," I said.

Neither of us spoke for a minute, and then Ann offered, sounding almost apologetic, "That's how we saw things then, how we talked about God."

"I can understand that," I said.

We wrapped up the visit soon after, and I thanked her profusely for her time. At home I put the photos she had given me on a shelf without looking at them further or showing them to Joe, uncertain what to feel or think about the encounter. I inhabited a cloud of confusion for several days until I could approach it again, this time with a researcher's mindset. What had I learned through this interview? Quite a lot, I concluded, about my mom in her 1950s college context, including specific places and some of the people. She had had friends and a social life. She had engaged in academic pursuits. She had dated and married in a particular era which may have circumscribed her choices in ways that seemed quite foreign to me.

Gut instinct had led me to conduct these interviews, without a clear idea of what I hoped to achieve. Now, I could see, they were steppingstones into my mom's life. Others' recollections allowed me to glean something of her experiences and personality, and I felt grateful to feel more acquainted with her.

Chapter Twenty-Eight

N ow I was on a roll and dug into the cache of photos from the condo that were still waiting to be sorted and shared among my siblings. Then it felt remarkably simple to call up my aunt Margie, widow of my mom's twin brother, and set up a visit to ask her about some of these items. I had never been to the apartment they'd moved to from their fifty-year home when my uncle Bill became too ill and infirm to do steps anymore.

"This is a great place! I really like it," I said following the brief tour, but Aunt Margie shook her head, dismissive. She would have rather stayed in her house.

The dining room was bright with afternoon sun coming in the picture window at our left as we sat down next to each other at the long table to peruse the photos I had brought. I began my now-familiar sequence of questions, starting with the origins of her relationship to my mom.

"I was classmates with a friend of your mom's from grade school. We were all three in a sorority together," she explained.

It was truly a revelation that Margie and my mom were friends long before Bill and Margie were a couple. Almost eerily like Joe and me getting together through Bitsy. I already knew that the house where my mom grew up was a social center for the young people. As Margie named a lot of the people in the high school photos, it reminded me of Ann's accounts of college—picnics, parties, overnights.

"Your mom was a serious student, disciplined and hardworking. She put her studies ahead of fun, especially during nursing school," Margie remembered, her expression grave. And yes, my mom did work at a hospital after she was married, Margie reported, though she couldn't say how long a time.

"I remember when she found the lump. She said it probably wasn't serious, then there was a plan to take care of it, and finally it was bad," Margie said, shaking her head, her eyes downcast with sorrow. "She felt sure that God wouldn't let her die because she had a blind child," she added.

Though I said nothing, my heart ached to hear this yet again. I remembered my mom as a devout Catholic, regularly attending weekday mass and praying the rosary daily. Her illness must have sparked a spiritual crisis. When I was in my thirties, especially if I had been facing advanced cancer as a mother of young children, I might have felt the same way. Now I was nearly twenty years older than my mom had been. I lived in a completely different time and held more nuanced beliefs. I trusted in divine presence, but not as an all-powerful being orchestrating my life's path. Had any priests visited my mom? If so, had she opened up to them about her fears? Or perhaps to one of her friends, like Mrs. Bowman? I recalled how Audrey, Ag's hospice nurse, had repeatedly offered conversational lifelines for her to share troubling thoughts, and her support team had also included a chaplain and a social worker.

Margie provided more detail about the day of my mom's death. At dinnertime my dad had taken the hospital's call saying that she had died. My mom's parents were present with us, and without any explanation my dad had said that he needed to run down to the hospital. Later that night, at their house, Margie answered the phone call from my grandpa, who just said, "It's over," and then hung up, so Margie had to tell Bill.

"Your mom's death was so sad for everyone," she said. "Just heartbreaking."

I told her what I had learned from Jeanne at lunch about my parents' deliberate disconnection from the Wimbergs, but she only said, "I never heard your grandparents say a bad word about Ag or Al, but it's possible they expressed those feelings in private."

When I was writing stories as a journalist, I usually determined that I had interviewed enough sources when they started saying similar things. In this vein, Margie's anecdotes reinforced what I'd learned from Rebecca and Ann from her own perspective. All the pieces fit together more coherently, creating a picture of my mom's life as warmly woven with relationships and animated by a drive for personal accomplishment. Realizing that Margie was the one living person of my acquaintance who had known my mom the longest, I felt grateful and relieved that I hadn't left it too late. Jeanne and Judy were so much younger that they had not been my mom's peers. Bill, her older brother Jim, and my dad were all gone.

Following this conversation, a Google search told me that the first hospice program in the United States was not established until 1974, four years after my mom's death. Clearly, she did not have those resources available. I also turned up information about Dr. Elisabeth Kubler-Ross. In 1969, the year before my mom died, she published *On Death and Dying*, which described the now-famous five stages of grief. Kübler-Ross's work began a shift in attitudes toward death, I learned, because she talked openly to the dying and their loved ones at a time when silence reigned.

Avoidance of difficult truth surely characterized my mom's illness and end of life, I thought, remembering her furtive research into her own symptoms to figure out that the cancer had spread to her brain. That took courage! It bothered me that my dad was not present when she died. Worried that she had been alone, I asked my older brother what he knew of that day.

"It was in the afternoon. Jim Bowman was the only one there. Her head hurt, so he was rubbing it, and then she died," he related, and I felt consoled.

After my cursory research on bereavement, I appreciated anew the pain that flowed through my aunts' accounts of my mom's disease and death, beneath my dad's anger, and within my grandma's listlessness. Our family's loss occurred just before a cultural tipping point on grief, and all of us suffered, young and old alike, because we could not talk about what we felt. We did not know how to, and there was no one to help us.

Next, I contacted my mom's high school and set up an appointment with Missy in the alumnae office. On the appointed morning, she met me at the front desk and led me down the hall to their office suite, where three yearbooks in plastic sleeves lay on a table in the middle of a large room that was clearly a workspace for the half dozen offices that opened off of it. Missy pointed to pictures on the wall of the previous school building on the property, torn down nearly two decades after my mom's tenure from 1948–1951, which provided helpful context.

"We only have three of her years here," she apologized, gesturing to the table, which deflated me. Then she consulted a coworker who assured us the library would have copies as well. Within a few minutes, the fourth one, for my mom's senior year, was added. By then I was already turning the pages of the freshman book and hit immediate pay dirt.

"My mom was president of the freshman class!" I said, pointing to the grouping of four officers, all of them dressed in white point-ed-collar blouses, dark A-line skirts below the knee, and saddle shoes with ankle socks. My mom wore her hair in a bob with barrettes high on either side, longer than in most pictures I had seen of her. I too had served on student council during high school but had never known of this invisible common thread between us.

When I pulled out my phone to photograph pages, Missy said, "I'm happy to copy any pages you like," and she handed me Post-it Notes to mark the desired ones. Elated to have a clear find, I con-tinued turning pages. The freshman yearbook was hardbound, like I think of a yearbook, but the other three were more like booklets and focused on the seniors, with just group shots of the other classes. From my mom's senior-year edition, I gathered that a girl named Jean was her close friend and that her intent to pur-sue nursing had already been declared.

At home that afternoon I perused the black-and-white pages again slowly, reading all the names. I paused multiple times on the student seated to my mom's left in the freshman-year group-ing. Something rang a bell. Finally, a Google search led to a 2003 obituary naming her as the mother of my high school classmate, Barb. The toothy smile and apple cheeks in the vintage copy sud-denly looked familiar. Studying the two mothers side by side and remembering Barb, I wondered if our yearbooks ever showed us next to each other.

All at once, heaviness descended like a stage curtain. Barb's mom had been there the whole time when I was younger, a mater-nal connection hiding in plain sight, but in high school I had been fully immersed in the new story where Ag was my mother. Back then, knowing our moms had been classmates might have meant little to me. Now, finding things could cut both ways. I loved knowing that I had followed my mom's path by serving on student council. It created a tangible link between us that I treasured. At the same time, the missed connection with my classmate's mom seemed to underscore all that was lost forever in the long decades between my mom's death and the present day, tempering the joy of discovery.

Adoption regret continued to percolate sporadically too. With little hope of finding the desired answer, still I kept Googling. Landing upon a new search term, "stepparent adoption," led to a definitive memo from the Ohio State Bar Association titled "Stepparent Adoption is Permanent." For some reason I kept going anyway, following related searches like "adoption laws" and "adoption records." Finally, "Ohio adoption records" brought reward of a sort on the Department of Health's site. Under a state law passed just a couple years earlier, records of adoptions that occurred between January 1, 1964, and September 18, 1996, were available, with proper identification, to adoptees and lineal descendants.

I clicked the link and read the home page several times. Yes, I fit all the required criteria. With a notarized form and a check for twenty dollars, I could receive a copy of my original birth certificate. Oh! The prospect of seeing my mom's name in official print brought a rush of anticipation. I gathered the needed items and sent them off in the mail. Less than two weeks later, a white #10 business envelope arrived at our house, much sooner than the estimated time stated on the website. It contained just three sheets of paper: a receipt documenting my request and payment, a gray photocopy of the original birth certificate, and a clear black-and-white copy of the adoption certificate dated December 15, 1975.

I held the birth certificate copy in trembling hands, just reading it again and again. *Mother: Mary Lee Wimberg.* The sting of tears signified so many emotions. Relief. Joy. Sorrow. This document could not bring her back any more than heirlooms or anecdotes about her life could, and neither could it serve as actual identification. Yet, without question, it attested to an essential part of my story. Its mere existence bolstered the narrative's credibility, like an eyewitness account suddenly rediscovered. While stories about my mom gave me inroads into her life, this birth certificate copy brought her tangibly back into mine. It made real what had become almost illusory.

A chance encounter with my cousin Theresa Wimberg, oldest child of my mom's older brother, took me even further into the past. She and I had always connected, despite sporadic contact through the years, maybe because we were born only two days apart. Though she attended a different school, her family had lived up the street on Principio when we moved there, so she had witnessed our "new" family in the making. I was sorry that they had moved less than a year after our arrival.

When I described my recent explorations and the questions that had arisen about Dad and Ag, she shared a unique angle of our family's evolution. "I actually talked to my dad about Al and Aggie once. I was curious. In the last years of his life, I was always asking him stuff," she said, adding wryly, "it was tough to get him to talk."

Uncle Jim was aware of his mom's hurt feelings after the remarriage but took a more moderate view, Theresa related. "He thought your dad just wanted to live his life," she said.

"Hmm, that's interesting," I said, adding this insight to my mental inventory.

She continued, thoughtful, "You know, I have a lot of pictures from Grandma and Grandpa, if you'd ever like to see them."

"I would love that!"

It took several months for us to get back together. On a late-autumn Saturday, we met at a public library, a central location but also a sentimental one, the branch nearest Principio that we had both patronized as kids. In the sloped parking lot behind the building, she lifted a large blue plastic tub from the trunk, and I reached in to grab the remaining shopping bags and stack of smaller plastic containers.

"Wow, there's a lot here!"

"Yes," she said. "I'm glad for a reason to look through it all again. It's been a while, one of those things I keep meaning to do."

We traipsed up the stairs to the back door and entered the children's area on the lower level, crossing through to the stairs up to the main level, both of us pointing out the decorative fountain and remembering where the copy machine had been, now an alcove with a table and chairs. After we settled at a round table near the back of the high-ceilinged room upstairs, Theresa opened the big bin first, filled with assorted portraits in frames, loose photos, and envelopes of varied sizes. Then, without fanfare, she began handing me things to look at.

I studied pictures of my grandparents at their wedding and blurry black-and-white images of my grandpa's sisters and mother, his stepmother actually, as Theresa reminded me, whispering. Soon the room around us faded away as we dug into photos of our parents' childhood in the 1930s, '40s, and '50s. The three oldest—her dad, my mom, and Bill—chubby-cheeked, standing together on the porch at about four and five years old. My mom and our grandma snuggled up next to each other in the bow of a rowboat. Later, the two younger sisters appeared as pigtailed little girls in matching outfits.

After a while, we barely even whispered, the only sounds the rustle of paper and my reflexive gasps at the exquisite beauty and innocence in these images of my mom as a child. Only a couple were at all familiar to me. Theresa urged me to choose any that I liked. "I've already set aside ones of my dad. Take what you want."

I felt like Indiana Jones entering the inner sanctum at the end of a long passageway as the stack of photos on the chair next to me continued to grow, a motherlode in every sense. Finally, I raised my eyes to Theresa's and said, "I think it was a happy childhood."

Her brown eyes met mine, her expression pensive as she considered, then said, "Yes . . . I think so too."

These photos filled me with amazement. I understood my mom much better now as a much-loved daughter and sister, nurtured by a mother who clearly delighted in all of them. Though my mom had died young and our connection was all but severed for many years, I still belonged to that lineage. I came from more than loss. I came from a loving maternal line. Unconsciously, I had already carried it forward with my own children. Now I was working to graft myself back to that original branch.

Chapter Twenty-Nine

A few months later, in a renovated church building set among the redwoods of northern California, a circle of padded folding chairs awaited at one end of the converted church with its vaulted ceiling and gleaming wood floors. In the center of the circle, a grouping of LED pillar candles of varying heights flickered gently. Feeling equal parts excited and scared, I joined the other women there for a motherless daughters retreat led by best-selling grief authors Hope Edelman and Claire Bidwell Smith.

At fifty-four, I had come prepared to be the oldest person, but the group ranged from twenty-two to sixty-nine years. All of us had lost our moms young, and, like me, most had had little or no opportunity, ever, to speak of their grief or connect with their mom's memory. Over the next four days, gathered in a circle, we told our stories of early loss.

My mother died of breast cancer when I was seven.

My mom had a brain aneurysm when I was sixteen.

My mom died when I was two.

My mom died in a car accident.

My mom died by suicide.

My mom died when I was eighteen; I cared for her through her illness starting at thirteen.

My mom was murdered.

There were no exclamations of pity or sorrow, only acceptance and head nods. Like veterans of fierce battle, we recognized the scars. Words were unnecessary.

On the second day, in a guided meditation, Claire set the scene for us to walk a path toward our younger selves. I immediately envisioned myself at seven years old in Minnesota where my family vacationed during my early childhood. I greeted my young self as she sat on a metal glider outside the cottage on a hill overlooking the lake. Sitting down next to her, I put my arm around her, held her close, and told her she was amazing. "I'm all grown up now and can handle it. You don't have to worry," I said, calmly and without tears.

The next day's meditation invited us down that same path and guided our present-day selves to encounter our mothers. Once again, my imagination went immediately to our vacation spot in Minnesota. This time I appeared as my middle-aged self, wearing that day's black leggings, long cardigan, and flowered scarf. I sat waiting, a little stiff and very uncertain. Then my mom approached from my right, smiling, radiating joy, a vivacious young mother dressed as she had been in my zoo memory from years ago, before cancer stole her vitality. She joined me on the glider, seating herself at the other end, respecting my resistance but undaunted by it. We were silent for a time as her gaze searched my face, until the warmth emanating from her reached me.

I said, "I miss you, and it was hard."

She responded only, "I know."

She made no move to hug me but instead reached over and squeezed my right hand, her eyes crinkled, and her lips pressed together in a pleased smile, long-forgotten gestures that all rang so true that I gasped. In my mind's eye, the bright afternoon sun intensified our connection as we continued to sit together with insects buzzing in the background. Time seemed suspended as I basked in her comforting presence. Too soon, Claire's voice broke in, prompting us to return to the present. Crying lightly, I allowed the image to gradually fade away.

As the subsequent days unfolded, we examined beliefs about ourselves that arose from being motherless; most prominently in my case: "I am broken." Delving further to find the truth of it, I discovered "broken" actually meant, "I feel unseen." There on the glider, greeted by my young mom, I had felt seen by her, and I think maybe she had felt seen by me.

In that circle of women, where we wept to acknowledge, yet again, the pain of all we had lost, we felt safe and known and seen. Among friends. Among sisters. A bond we had never experienced before. Even after all these years, still there were new depths to plumb. I had never been in a group of motherless women before. To discover that abandonment issues, hypervigilance, and over-responsibility were normal among us, to begin teasing each other about it even, was life changing. I experienced a sense of belonging previously beyond my imagination. Real-life bonding far surpassed anything a book could ever provide.

Back home again the following week, I sat at our dining room table surrounded by dozens of photos from the family collection. I had been procrastinating about dividing these with my siblings. Now, buoyed by newfound connection to my mom and to other motherless daughters, this step came naturally, part of putting broken pieces back into a whole.

A snapshot from 1968 showed my mom and me sitting on the dock in Minnesota, the day sunny but probably breezy too, because I was snuggled up to her wrapped in an adult-size white terrycloth beach cover-up. The short sleeves came to my elbows, the length covered my knees and shins, and my arms were clasped loosely around my middle, holding the two sides closed. My mom wore a blue-patterned one-piece bathing suit. Her slender figure looked relaxed. Loose dark curls topped her face, and she smiled sweetly into the camera as though there was no other place she would rather be. Closer examination showed that I was smiling too, but my round face was angled down, possibly admiring the cover-up, imagining myself grown-up and stylish, or just feeling the warm fabric against my skin. I sensed the rough-ridged wood of the dock and the damp sand beneath our feet. Behind us, the green pine trees rose up against the blue sky, and below there was shallow brownish-green water and the tan sand with a bit of grass growing up in a few places. The photo showed us sitting at a threshold of time as well as place. A month later, just before my fifth birthday, my mother would be diagnosed with breast cancer.

An envelope held a set of five-by-sevens showing each of us with our mom in her final summer, on a pontoon boat ride in Minnesota. The cancer photos, I called them; I had avoided them. I surmised that Dad intentionally took each one. Had he realized her time was finite, or was it an unconscious act? I considered how he had to go back through the negatives to find these particular photos and take them somewhere to be developed, drop them off and return a week later for the prints, a lot more involved than simply uploading from a mobile device. I hoped the gesture brought solace to him as a forty-year-old widowed father.

In two weeks' time, all my siblings would join me around the table to pore over these photos and divide them up. The time had arrived to release these vintage photos into the world, to claim my choices and let the rest go. To prepare, I was grouping them chronologically as best as possible and selecting which ones to copy for myself ahead of the gathering. In this surge of activity, I recognized the hypervigilant child and the capable adult smoothing the way for self and others, embracing myself now as both and relaxing into the loving expression of my organizational talents.

I wondered about the pleasure these early childhood photos inspired. Did ignorance of the real events they documented allow me to color them rosy without ambivalence? Like bringing circulation back to frostbitten extremities, they seemed to reactivate something nearly lost. It felt dreamy and cozy to drop down into that world before a thirty-seven-year-old mom's death left her husband and four children adrift, until remarriage and adoption nearly erased her memory. Surely there were issues and fractures back then too, but I was too young to understand much. The pictures evoked my childhood innocence almost as a physical sensation. Much sorrow had ensued, but thankfulness for the time before, with my mom, washed over me.

On the actual sorting day, I sat at the head of the table by the buffet, my usual spot at holidays. Tim and then Kate were to my right, Mike and Mark on the left. I had plotted the order of business like lots at an auction. Ag's jewelry first, dispatched mostly to Mark, though Kate and I each received a few items. Then a box of mementoes from our dad's parents, which detoured into much speculation about great-uncles and great-aunts we had never known, examining nearly century-old photos of our dad's parents and their siblings.

When we embarked on the pre-1974 photos, I suggested to Mark that he go to the family room and begin reviewing Ag's album collection, which had resided on our bookshelf since the condo clear-out more than a year earlier. He pulled up a kitchen chair and paged through the albums one by one, while in the dining room, expectancy reigned, unspoken, as a chamber stood ready for opening. I placed piles of loose photos in the center and summarized the organization system.

"I already made digital copies of the ones I really want. In general, I think people should claim ones of themselves, don't you? And we can make more copies of certain ones if needed," I said.

The quiet of a research library permeated the room, broken at intervals by spontaneous, hushed exclamations.

"Look at this," someone would say, holding out a poignant image of a new baby in arms, toddlers in a play pool, or a child blowing out birthday candles.

"Oh, wow, I haven't thought of this in years," was said of a sports team or a bicycle or a trip.

Kate sat taking it all in, albeit without seeing. Intermittently someone would describe a picture to her.

I said, "Kate, I'm putting aside ones of you." Even though she could not see them herself, maybe she'd like to share her story with a friend or coworker sometime.

"Thanks, Peg," she replied.

Without speaking, at points I passed the tissues to Mike and then Tim, each choking up at different moments, seeing our young mom. In the end the pictures practically sorted themselves it seemed. Everyone had a pile. Hours had passed while we were engrossed, and now everyone was hungry and tired, though smiling in contentment. Consideration of Ag's albums would have to wait for another time.

Not long after the afternoon with my siblings, I entered Dr. Jackson's office for my monthly appointment. We each settled into our places following the usual pleasantries, and before she could even land an anticipatory look, I said hurriedly, "I want to talk to Ag today."

"Well! Okay then," she replied, leaning back with her eyebrows raised.

"I know, when you suggested it, it made me afraid," I said, recalling the pit of terror that had opened at the mere thought of such an imagined conversation. "Driving over here, thinking about what to discuss today, it just came to me that I want to. It's time."

Nodding her understanding, Dr. Jackson gestured toward the vacant club chair to her right, across from the couch where I sat. "Should she be here?"

"I suppose so," I replied.

Feeling a little ridiculous, but determined, I directed my gaze to the chair and waited to see if Ag appeared in any way. After a minute, I envisioned an older version of her, not near death, but a paler, receded image of the woman who had intimidated me so profoundly. She sat still, looking past me.

I dove in before nerve could desert me. "I need to tell you that I was very hurt by things you did." Then I enumerated my grievances, starting with the guest towels and continuing through the household demands, the mirrored tray, and the extended family distancing.

"I just don't understand how you could do these things. Your own dad died when you were a baby. How could you not understand the importance of a dead parent's heirlooms? And I know you didn't act alone to cut me off from the Wimbergs—Dad was part of that—but that's really the worst of all. I'd already lost my mother, and then I lost her again."

After a minute, Dr. Jackson asked, "What would you want her to say?"

"I don't really know. We didn't speak directly to one another, especially about our feelings. Once, during high school, I tried to unburden myself to her about things, and all I got in return was how hard it was for her because Dad worked so much. Then, on her deathbed, she tried to tell me something, but it was unintelligible."

"Hmm." We both waited until I found words.

Another silence was followed by a new revelation. "I've

puzzled for nearly two years now over what she tried to say to me just before she died. 'I want to love you' I think is what she said, which sounds good, but I felt uneasy afterward, not comforted at all. I realize now it was the tone that bothered me. Even declining toward death, it sounded a lot like when I was in high school—as if she were justifying herself. So, what I would really want is for her to say, 'I'm sorry,' full stop, no excuses or deflections."

Dr. Jackson nodded once, then knitted her brows. "Do you think she did it on purpose to hurt you? Of course, she did hurt you, but was that her intent, do you think?"

She had asked this question before, nearly a year earlier when I'd first returned to her office after more than twenty-five years, following the lunch with Jeanne and Judy. Then, I had managed only a listless "I don't know."

Letting her words sink in, reflecting, I discovered that today felt different. I exhaled a puff of air and said, "No, I don't think she intended to hurt me. I think it must have come from insecurity. In my gut, I think possibly she wanted what her friends had. She had been in the convent for fifteen years while they were starting families. This was her chance to have that ready-made, and she was always a person for whom appearances meant a great deal. Also, maybe she was threatened by my mom's memory, and she needed to assert her position. I can't relate to this, but that's how I see her. She did hurt me very much."

We sat again without speaking.

"If I had to boil it down," I continued, "I'd just say to her, 'You never saw me.'" Turning toward the vacant chair, I said, "You never saw me as the desperate, wounded child that I was, who needed tender care."

Still more pushed to the surface. Addressing Dr. Jackson, I said, "There were good things she brought to my life—shopping for clothes, learning how to give a dinner party, that feminine stuff that many motherless women feel they missed—I did receive them from her, and I'm grateful . . . but that doesn't change the harm that she caused, that she and Dad caused, by separating me from my mom's family."

Dr. Jackson leaned on the chair arm, her chin on her fist as I continued.

"I remember the night Ag died, how Mark stayed in the chair next to the bed, holding her hand, kissing her forehead from time to time. He was Ag's purest relationship, I think, her child that she birthed, the person she loved unconditionally. On that, I can relate to her, the primal force of loving our children, but our maternal lives ran parallel to each other, never really intersected."

During this stream of insights, my limbs stayed loose, and no tears burned.

"Recently I looked through Ag's photo albums, and they meant little to me."

I became quiet, and Dr. Jackson asked, "Why do you think that's the case?"

After pondering for a moment, I replied, "Those books are not my story. They're hers. I have my own pictures of Mark through the years that I treasure. But I'm living my own story. She had a part in it for a long time, but that's in the past. I'm ready to set it down now."

The sureness in my own voice caught me off guard. I had not expected to say these words, but they were true. My whole body responded with ease as I settled further into my seat.

"I'm happy for you," she said, sitting back in the chair, smiling.

"Me too," I said. "Thanks."

At last, after years and years of free-falling, I had landed in my life.

In this more peaceful state of being, my imagination meandered on its own through different scenarios in which Ag and I were open with one another. What would it have been like to hear her share about never having known her father? Could we then have spoken about Mary Lee, perhaps even acknowledged her as a key link in the family chain? A twinge of regret for this alternate possibility flared briefly, but I let it pass.

Chapter Thirty

Spring had arrived. Eagerly I presented the necklace for inspection at the jewelry store. The chain was tarnished to a dark brown, but the heart-shaped pendant, with its tiny painted rose, still gleamed. While integrating heirlooms from the condo, this long-ago gift from Ag had resurfaced in my top drawer, and I'd instantly known what I would do.

"I want to give it to my niece for her first communion," I explained to the saleswoman.

"It's very pretty," she said, using tiny pliers to detach the little heart before taking the chain to the back for cleaning.

As I wandered among the glass-topped display cases, my thoughts turned to Shannon, now in second grade and about to turn eight years old. Months earlier, I had attended grandparents' day at her school. Arriving at her classroom, I had pulled up a chair alongside her desk as the other visitors had done. Though I had detected a small smile, she had kept her head bowed over her tasks, her body unusually rigid. Eventually the teacher had called the group to order and invited us to introduce ourselves. As the process moved around the room, I had noticed that I was the only non-grandparent in attendance, though no one remarked on it.

Then the teacher explained that the children had made name tags, and each had a set of interview questions. The noise level rose as this activity got underway, but Shannon stayed hunched over her papers, still not looking up at me.

Trying to sound nonchalant, I had waited a moment before asking, "Do you want to interview me?"

"Those are for grandparents," she had said, which had stung even as I'd recalled from my own children's growing up the literalness of their thinking at this stage.

Then I had spied two laminated name tags on string peeking out from beneath her papers. They read "Nana" and "Papa," her grandparents in Canada, her mom's parents, and a likely explanation had begun to form in my mind. The teacher probably had instructed her to make name tags for her grandparents, so she did. They were her only living grandparents now. I had wondered if Mark and Laura had missed the memo that only grandparents were invited to this day, or if it was an unwritten bit of institutional knowledge that they hadn't yet possessed.

Growing more uncomfortable, I'd sat another minute wishing I could vanish, until my peripheral vision caught sight of Shannon as if at a distance but also laser focused. I saw an intelligent, sensitive little girl who had lost her only nearby grandparent, with whom she had visited often and who had doted on her. She was a grieving child. The lens then turned toward myself, a middle-aged adult leaning toward the happy-ending version of the story, where I would step in seamlessly as a beloved grandma for Shannon, replacing Ag in the narrative by opening a new chapter on a blank page.

From the time of Shannon's birth, I had harbored hope that this role might one day fall to me, given Ag's elder age. Over the years I had nurtured my own bond with Shannon by babysitting her periodically at their house and ours. Once, when she was four and I picked her up at daycare, another child had sized me up as I signed in and asked, "Are you Shannon's grandma?" Standing next to me, Shannon had hooted at the idea, but unmistakable delight had rippled through me. I'd had a terrific grandma, and though our relationship had been sadly truncated, I'd rejoiced for that brief instant of identifying with her.

On that grandparents day, seated next to Shannon in the chaotic classroom, I'd glanced again at the interview paper and envisioned myself smiling brightly and cajoling Shannon, "Oh, but I'm here. You can interview me. Just ask me the questions," while picking up the sheet and placing it in front of her. The imagined interaction jolted me. No, grieving children need truth.

Instead, I'd asked, "Can we work on the word search together? I think they're fun to do."

Bingo. Her entire being had melted, and hazel eyes sparkled up at me with her familiar grin so like Mark's. Tossing her long braid over her shoulder, she had pointed to the list of words yet to be located and slid the paper between us. We had chatted and giggled in a companionable cocoon until the teacher called us to the next activity.

That experience had provided another important piece in my reassembled story. I was not her grandma; I was her aunt. Seeing her loss and confusion, I had chosen real discomfort over a fake happy ending. That had felt right, liberating even. It's what I would have wanted at her age. Giving her the necklace from Ag arose from the same impulse.

The jewelry saleswoman had been gone for a while, I realized with a start. Just then she appeared from the back of the store, shaking her head. "I just can't get it to shine," she said. "Would you like to buy a new one?"

None of the replacement options she offered possessed the delicacy that I had always liked about the original, which disappointed me. Ultimately, I chose a simple gold box-style chain. With the rose charm attached, the overall effect was different than before, but refreshed and ready for a new generation, I had to admit. An elegant gray box with a matching bow completed the package and the process. At home, I placed it in a small gift bag covered with pink and purple pansies and wrote a card.

The following weekend Joe and I arrived early to the church for the first communion mass. Walking down the aisle, we passed through puddles of color created by sunshine streaming through the stained glass. Their family's pew, Mark had texted, was the second on the right, confirmed by the homemade felt banner hung on the side. Eyeing the thick pillar at the far end, which cut off at least two seats, and tallying up the possible attendees, we planted ourselves in a different pew, just behind the center reserved section, as a helpful gesture to cover any gaps. In my mind, we would hold these seats as a favor and then claim our rightful place in the reserved pew, but while I waited in line at the restroom and then chatted with an acquaintance in the vestibule, others in our group occupied the final two spots I would have considered "ours."

Returning down the aisle, the church now reverberating with conversation, I saw the full pew that now excluded us, and the strongest wave of abandonment I had experienced in a very long time crashed over me. As I slid past Joe to return to what was clearly to be my permanent seat for the mass, the two of us now a lone outpost, my heart pounded, and the tears I tried to choke back pooled in my eyes. I wanted to run out of church. I wanted to sob aloud. I wanted to calm down. I grabbed Joe's hand and squeezed it hard, leaning my forehead on his shoulder for a moment.

"What's wrong?" he asked, concerned.

"I'm feeling really bad. Sitting here alone. . . ."

"Ohh," he said.

I whispered, "I don't know what to do. I need something. I'm coming undone."

The strains of organ music began as I slid my phone from my purse. Holding it low, off to my left, hoping no one would notice, I quickly tapped out a message to the motherless daughters retreat group: "Feeling majorly triggered at niece's first communion. Good vibes needed." After hitting "send" to seek connection, my heart began to slow.

At niece's first communion. First communion. Mentally, the words lit up in neon. Of course. My first communion had taken place just six months after my mom died. Even when I wasn't conscious of it, loss lived in me. I surreptitiously peeked at my phone as I stood for the procession. Only two minutes had passed, but already two replies had appeared:

"Understandable, Peg. I'm here. Holding you in my heart."

"Sending you love."

Joe leaned over and whispered, "If it makes any difference, I'm genuinely more comfortable here. We have more room and a better view."

Nodding, I pressed his hand, then opened the hymnal to join the singing and wait for Shannon to come up the aisle looking so sweet in her white dress and veil. Back at their house, after a leisurely lunch, Laura's mom and sister began presenting their gifts, so I added my small bag to the queue and joined them in the circle around Shannon as she opened them. When my turn came, Shannon first pulled the card from the envelope and read it aloud:

Blessings and best wishes on your first communion day! This gift comes to you with much love. Your Grandma Morse received it at her baptism. She gave it to me, and now it will be yours. It gives me great joy to pass it down to you.

Love, Aunt Peg

"Oh, it's beautiful!" Laura said when Shannon opened the gray box. Then she unhooked the chain and fastened it around Shannon's neck, the tiny click shifting major pieces of my story into their proper places.

"Thanks, Peg. That really means a lot," Mark said, leaning over to hug me.

"You're welcome. It means a lot to me too," I replied, embracing him in return.

Shannon and I posed for a picture on the wide ottoman in their family room, snuggled together and grinning widely, the four fruit prints hanging on the wall behind us.

Two weeks later, I drove six hours to St. Louis to attend a motherless daughters luncheon organized by my retreat friend Melanie. Another retreat friend, Sarah, had driven from Michigan. On the morning of the event, the empty café hummed with nervous energy as time ticked toward the eleven o'clock start. Melanie darted about talking to staff, setting up centerpieces, arranging the sign-in table. I stood with a mug of dark roast coffee pondering the mural of lemon tree branches that spanned the entire back wall above black wainscoting. Bright-yellow plastic chairs at two long tables accented the lemons' lushness. Overall, an inviting space for twenty motherless women to gather for lunch on the day before Mother's Day.

For Melanie's sake, if no other reason, I wanted this inaugural luncheon to go well. She asked Sarah and me to assist with mingling, to make sure everyone was included in conversation during that chasm between arrival and sitting down for lunch. We shared a hope that the women who came today could find a measure of the connection we forged at the retreat, aware that we had had four days, and this event was two hours.

The first to enter was a young woman in her mid-twenties, who after being greeted took a seat on the cushiony couch just inside the door. A couple others came in together soon after, so I sat down next to the first person and struck up a conversation about her graduate degree and career plans. My having traveled from Cincinnati to the event sparked interest.

"Wow, that's so cool!" she said.

"Sarah, Melanie, and I met at a motherless daughters retreat back in January. When Melanie decided to do this, I kind of impulsively said I'd come. There isn't an event like this in Cincinnati that I know of, and I didn't feel like organizing one," I replied.

I had been wracking my brain for a smooth entry into *How'd your mother die?* Perhaps this mention of the retreat would suffice.

Uncrossing my legs, I turned slightly to face her and tried to sound casual. "My mom died when I was seven of breast cancer. . . . If you don't mind my asking, what's your mother-loss story?"

"My mom died of cancer too, when I was twelve," she said. Her face went slack as she looked down and away.

"Oh, okay," I said, sinking back into the couch cushions. "Well, how did you hear about the lunch today?"

"I saw it on Facebook," she replied, her relief at the redirection reflected in the eyes that met mine now.

A little while later, after we moved to the lunch tables, I tried again with a woman in her thirties on my left, Cara. "What brought you here today? If you don't mind my asking, what's your mother-loss story?"

She leaned closer, her wide blue eyes earnest. "She died very suddenly, in a freak accident, about ten years ago."

Such forthrightness caught the attention of the two women across the table, and when Cara finished speaking, someone else picked right up telling their story. With a Mona Lisa smile, Sarah nodded almost imperceptibly from down the table. Yes, I sensed it too. We were accomplishing our purpose. It was a strange, heady feeling to lead others in sharing about mother loss after nearly a lifetime of not talking about it. I had traveled so much farther than the three hundred miles from Cincinnati to reach this point, across decades of confusion, through layer upon layer of grief, to uncover my truth and tell it.

Back at Melanie's house afterward, I removed a hardbound eight-and-a-half-by-eleven-inch book from the tote bag in which it had traveled. Bold turquoise block letters on the front cover said *Mary Lee Wimberg Morse 1933–1970, Family Life in Pictures*. I had used an online service to compile images from my cousin's and my family's archive. While clicking and cropping to arrange the pages, several times I had begun composing descriptive text, but I halted each time after a sentence or two. Language felt inadequate; the pictures spoke for themselves. In the end, I had included only brief identifying captions. From the moment I unwrapped the flat box that arrived a week after I had pressed "submit" on the finished book, I knew that merely possessing it would never be enough. I needed to share it.

"Could I show you pictures of my mom? Are you okay with that? I know it can be painful for some motherless daughters if they don't have photos of their mom."

"Absolutely!" "Let me see that!" They both exclaimed at the same time. Melanie held it while Sarah looked over her shoulder.

"Peg, this is beautiful," Melanie said.

"Thanks. I just love how sweet she looked as a baby," I said with equal parts pride, ease, and joy, sensations that were growing in familiarity. Twice recently I had brought "the Mary Lee book" in its protective tote to share with friends over lunch and, like today, waited for an opportune moment to say, "Can I show you something?"

"I want to do this too!" Sarah crowed.

I departed St. Louis early the next morning to be home for a Mother's Day dinner that Joe and Kieran were planning. Upon arrival, I created a display in the front hall with the book, flowers cut from the yard, and a framed portrait of my mom in her wedding dress, seated on the piano bench at her family's home. Before dinner, Tim and I sat side by side in a glider on our deck as he paged through the book. After the sequence showing her childhood, young adulthood, and wedding, there was a page for each of her four children.

"I remember that day, that boat ride," Tim said, pointing to the one of our mom and me that I call the cancer photo.

"I kind of do too," I said. "It used to be too painful for me to look at this picture, but now it seems important to do. She looks terribly ill, and I look so young and innocent. I like seeing us both as we were."

Next came two composite pages, and I pointed to a picture of Tim and me, about three and five, perched on the edge of a plastic pool on the back patio at Raeburn. "My favorite—an icon of our early childhood. This image conjures for me all the time we spent playing together around the house."

Laughing, we both recalled how after our mom died, no one could ever assemble that pool again.

"I'd see it in the garage and ask about it. Dad always said, 'It doesn't have all the parts. We can't use it.'" Tim said.

When he came to the last page, I explained, "I chose each of these pictures for a reason. This one shows all her grandchildren, including Shannon too. And this one—of Judy and Kieran at her graduation—it symbolizes the maternal line being reconnected."

But there was still more. He might have missed it if I hadn't pointed out the clear plastic pocket affixed to the inside back cover. "See, in here is a photocopy of my original birth certificate."

I removed the paper from the pocket, handed it to him to

unfold, and knew exactly when he read the words "Mother: Mary Lee Wimberg." Our eyes smiled in unison as another piece fit into place.

A month later, Joe wound the car over the cemetery's smooth blacktop roadways to our long-established parking place just past my mom's grave. Twice annually now, we made this pilgrimage. For a long time, it was only in November, near my mom's death anniversary, but with little conscious thought, we'd added a June visit over the past few years. I made a private game of trying to spot her stone as we approached. The ground had shifted in the nearly three decades since our astounding first visit, so I had to watch carefully, but my eyes found it after a minute.

Keeping with our tradition, we stood several moments, not speaking, before the stone that reads "Mary Lee Morse, 1933–1970." Then, crouching down, I placed a small bunch of lavender and roses I had cut from our yard onto the grave marker. We stayed a little longer in amiable silence. The persistent, unquenchable longing—to find my mom, to know her, to be with her even just for a minute—washed over me lightly as I looked at her name on the ground. As it passed like a wave, I reached for Joe's hand.

"Ready?" he said, and I nodded my agreement.

Together we stepped around my mom's grave and began walking away from it through the grass, all the way across the section in which she is buried, past the lone tree in the center of it. When we reached the road on the other side, we turned right briefly and then left. I did not recollect so precisely where Dad and Ag were buried, but I knew they were close to the road about halfway down. The separate plots had been heartbreaking at the time of Dad's death five years earlier, but discovering the ability to walk between them easily had brought solace. Now Ag had been gone for two years.

"There they are," Joe said, pointing and leading me over. Once again, we stood without speaking, and I read the names and years to myself. Both of their death anniversaries are in mid-June, which sparked this additional visit in our calendar. I did not bring flowers for these graves, not because of any hard feelings, but from the simple recognition that I had had years of relationship with each of them, had actively engaged with their deaths, including intentional goodbyes, and remembered them fully. With my mom, I am always working to rebuild memory, and mindful gestures help to restore her rightful role in my story. A mix of emotions began to stir as I gazed downward, all the familiar angst and resentment and sorrow, too, at what might have been. Squeezing Joe's hand and feeling my feet firmly on the ground, I allowed these feelings to appear and then exhaled, releasing them to the breeze.

As we strolled back to the car, circling around via the road this time, the fact of distance between their graves requiring movement from one to another suddenly seemed quite fitting. To understand my loss in its many facets and then reassemble my story had required me to journey across a wide chasm and, of necessity, to accept a certain lasting gap in the narrative. Depending on the moment or the day, this breach could trigger sadness, anger, or shame in any combination. I had claimed these emotions not only as ongoing threads in my story but also as valued parts of myself. Over many years, I had worked and worked them until they wove together, if not perfectly, at least well enough, discovering along the way that I would rather live this truth than pretend anything else. Excavating my past to reconstruct a narrative for the present would continue, I was certain, even as the future was already arriving, because early loss never stops echoing.

Epilogue

When my turn came, I introduced myself following the group's time-honored custom: "My name is Peg. My mom died. And my favorite ice cream is vanilla." The process continued with my cofacilitator, Sandy, and our six-to-eight-year-old participants to start off the twice-monthly grief support meeting. Elsewhere in the building, other age groups as well as adults were gathering too. We'd all had pizza together before dispersing. It was a typical evening at Fernside Center for Grieving Children and Families in Cincinnati.

Tonight, our group of eight would do an activity around the theme of Telling the Story, chosen from the three-inch resource binder that facilitators receive. Sandy and I passed out blank sheets of paper with lines drawn to create six equal boxes and placed bags of markers and colored pencils in the center of the table.

Calling everyone to attention, Sandy explained the activity and began the instructions. "In the first box, at the top, I want you to write this heading: 'What Happened.' Then draw or write a few words about what happened to your person who died."

After the typical hubbub while everyone grabbed their preferred color of marker and got started, most of the kids settled into creating an image, some of them quite engrossed. At my very first experience with this program, observing a group prior to my volunteer training, I was blown away that "telling the story" mattered so much as to merit a whole category of activities, its own tab in the binder, a discovery I found freeing. After all I had been through to claim my story, these resonated the most.

We continued to lead the children through five more headings: How You Found Out, Funeral, Back at School, What Changed, and Favorite Memory. When most people finished, we invited them to share about their drawings, and as each child spoke in turn, Sandy and I offered head nods and occasional queries to the group as a whole: "Did anybody else feel that way when they returned to school?"

I had heeded intuition when I signed up as a volunteer here. Upon completing the four-week training course, I opted to begin as a floater, two Monday nights per month, helping where needed rather than committing to a specific age group. At the time, I worried a lot about executing activities properly and saying the right thing, so a gradual immersion seemed preferable. Then a facilitator spot opened in this group several months later. Would I be willing to fill it? Suddenly, I absolutely wanted to work with kids the very age I had been when my mom died.

Tonight, when the eight-year-old girl to my immediate right recounted seeing her mom's body just after death, her words came haltingly, and her voice quavered and rose almost as if she were asking rather than telling. *She's piecing the story together*, I realized, perhaps for the first time. The death had occurred only three months earlier. My heart squeezed in recognition, but this wasn't about me. It was a sacred moment for another young girl that I was privileged to witness. Exhaling softly, I felt my body supported in the chair, my hands loose in my lap as I steadied my neutral gaze on her face. When she finished, I simply said, "Thank you for sharing your story with us."

The children in this group have taught me that "doing it right" is more about being present than doing things a certain way. Since death follows no timetable, new children can join at any point. Often, they arrive downcast and quiet, and as facilitators, we watch for the telltale shift. It can take a few sessions. Maybe it occurs during the introductions, hearing the litany of "my mom died" or "my dad died," or maybe it occurs while another child relates what happened or describes a favorite memory of the person who died or just says aloud how much they miss them. The new child's shoulders lower ever so slightly or their eyes soften just a bit to discover they are not alone.

And then they begin to speak.

Acknowledgments

This book results from the lengthy, interwoven processes of grieving and writing. Starting it, much less finishing, required varied support over many years. Donna Jackson, PhD, posed the thorny questions that ultimately provoked the necessary introspection. "Promptress" Jena Schwartz and the Creative Ease writing community lit the narrative spark. Marion Roach Smith offered key insights on structure at the midpoint. Finally, with her unique blend of kindness, wisdom, and editorial acumen, Nadine Kenney Johnstone guided me to craft the story I longed to tell.

Along the way, Hope Edelman's groundbreaking work, and later her personal warmth, led to insights and connections far richer than anything I had ever imagined. Because of Hope and Claire Bidwell Smith, I can send boundless thanks to the January 2018 Dragonflies and the Fly It Forward women for sisterhood as motherless daughters. I also appreciate the Healing Power of Stories book group and the larger virtual communities of motherless daughters and adults bereaved as children that provide ongoing validation, as well as Allison K. Williams and Ashleigh Renard of the Writers Bridge, for modeling authenticity and generosity as the foundation of authorship, and Brooke Warner and the She Writes Press team, for bringing my book into the world.

I cannot adequately thank my husband, Joe. His unconditional love and unflagging encouragement fuel all my endeavors. Lastly, with deepest gratitude, I acknowledge my children, siblings, and extended family, with special thanks to my daughter, Kieran, for her understanding and love.

About the Author

Peg Conway earned a master's in journalism and worked in corporate communication before focusing on raising her family. Now she writes and practices energy healing in Cincinnati, OH, where she also volunteers at a children's grief center. Her essays about early mother loss and long-term grieving have appeared at *The Manifest-Station*, the *Cincinnati Enquirer*, and The Mighty. Peg and her husband have three grown children and one grandchild.

Reading Group Discussion Guide

1. What do you think motivated the author to tell her story?

2. The long-term, lifelong nature of grief is a central theme in this book. To what extent do you relate to that idea? How has it manifested in your life?

3. How would you describe children's grief after reading this author's experience? How does it differ from adults'? What are the most important needs of a grieving child?

4. The impulse to impose a "happy ending" rather than face painful truth occurs several times. What is the cost of choosing the former? What makes it possible to choose the latter? How have you experienced this sort of challenge?

5. The author struggles to accept the wounded parts of herself. How does she offer herself compassion?

6. Discuss the theme of finding one's story as presented in this narrative. What is the connection between the story we tell about ourselves and our identity?

7. What kind of person is Ag? Discuss her strengths and weaknesses and her influence on the author. What is her legacy to the author?

8. Comment on the role of the author's father in her life. What are his strengths and weaknesses? What is his legacy to the author?

9. What resources and strengths does the author draw on as a child, young adult, wife/mother, and in middle age to cope with her situation? What was the most significant factor in her ability to grieve and heal?

10. What event(s) in the story resonated the most for you?

11. This book reflects the evolution of cancer treatment, end-of-life care, and bereavement support since the mid-twentieth century. What changes in any of these areas have impacted your life? What improvements are still needed?

12. Are objects and heirlooms of the past important to you? Why or why not? If yes, describe one of them. What story does it tell?

SELECTED TITLES FROM SHE WRITES PRESS

She Writes Press is an independent publishing
company founded to serve women writers everywhere.
Visit us at www.shewritespress.com.

Veronica's Grave: A Daughter's Memoir by Barbara Bracht Donsky. $16.95,
978-1-63152-074-7. A loss and coming-of-age story that follows young
Barbara Bracht as she struggles to comprehend the sudden disappearance
and death of her mother and cope with a blue-collar father intent upon
erasing her mother's memory.

The Butterfly Groove: A Mother's Mystery, A Daughter's Journey by Jessica Barraco. $16.95, 978-1-63152-800-2. In an attempt to solve the mystery of
her deceased mother's life, Jessica Barraco retraces the older woman's
steps nearly forty years earlier—and finds herself along the way.

Splitting the Difference: A Heart-Shaped Memoir by Tré Miller-Rodríguez.
$19.95, 978-1-938314-20-9. When 34-year-old Tré Miller-Rodríguez's
husband dies suddenly from a heart attack, her grief sends her on an
unexpected journey that culminates in a reunion with the biological
daughter she gave up at 18.

Where Have I Been All My Life? A Journey Toward Love and Wholeness by Cheryl
Rice. $16.95, 978-1-63152-917-7. Rice's universally relatable story of
how her mother's sudden death launched her on a journey into the deepest parts of grief—and, ultimately, toward love and wholeness.

The First Signs of April: A Memoir by Mary-Elizabeth Briscoe. $16.95, 978-
1631522987. Briscoe explores the destructive patterns of unresolved
grief and the importance of connection for true healing to occur in this
inspirational memoir, which weaves through time to explore grief reactions to two very different losses: suicide and cancer.

I Know It In My Heart: Walking through Grief with a Child by Mary E. Plouffe.
$16.95, 978-1-631522-00-0. Every child will experience loss; every
adult wants to know how to help. Here, psychologist Mary E. Plouffe
uses her own family's tragic loss to tell the story of childhood grief—its
expression and its evolution—from ages three to fifteen.